CW00642322

THE RECORDER

Stephen F. Goodyear

B.E.M., B.Sc.(Econ.), A.R.C.M.
Author of the 'New Recorder Tutor' series

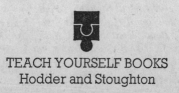

TEACH YOURSELF BOOKS
Hodder and Stoughton

First impression 1978

Copyright © 1978 Stephen F. Goodyear

Published in the U.S.A. by David McKay & Co. Inc., 750 Third Avenue, New York, N.Y. 10017, U.S.A.

British Library CIP Data
Goodyear, Stephen F
    The Recorder. – (Teach yourself books).
    1. Recorder (Musical instrument).
    I. Title
    788'.53'0712   MT340
    ISBN 0–340–22247–6

ISBN 0 340 22247 6

Printed and bound in Great Britain for
Hodder and Stoughton Paperbacks,
a division of Hodder and Stoughton Ltd,
Mill Road, Dunton Green, Sevenoaks, Kent
(Editorial Office: 47 Bedford Square, London WC1B 3DP)
by Hazell Watson & Viney Ltd, Aylesbury, Bucks

Contents

Foreword

This book has been a labour of love. I have always been interested in the technique of teaching the recorder, and in the challenge of producing a book which would help aspiring players as a teacher would, yet without going too far.

Knowledge of teaching does not always come from books and instruction, but also from the study of pupils. I would therefore like to thank all my pupils, past and future, but in particular Ben Mayo. Nor must I forget Lydia Greeves, for her help in turning a vast and ill-coordinated manuscript into something which I hope will be of use to many people; Nicholas Raine, of the Bournemouth Symphony Orchestra, who wrote out the musical illustrations; Myles Cooper of Lymington, who took the photographs; and last, and most of all, my wife Dee, who puts up so gallantly with the manifold disadvantages of having a writer for a husband.

Acknowledgements

The author wishes to thank the following publishers for permission to use various extracts:

    Messrs Schott & Co. Ltd., 48, Great Marlborough Street, London, for:

        Telemann, Trio-Sonata in D minor; Yugoslav Dance, *arr.* Allen;

        Dowland, The Earl of Essex Galliard;

        Couperin/Dolmetsch, Le Rossignol en Amour.

    Messrs Belwin-Mills Music Ltd., 250 Purley Way, Croydon, for:

        Greek Air.

    Bayerische Staats-Bibliothek, Munich, for:

        Phalese, Schiazura Marazula.

The remainder of the quotations come from original sources in the author's collection.

Introduction

When you decided to learn a musical instrument, somewhere in your mind must have been the question, 'Can I make a success of it?'

Much depends on your definition of success. If you mean 'Can I enjoy myself making music, and give pleasure to others?', then the answer is probably 'Yes'. If you mean 'Can I become the world's foremost player?' then the answer is, with a very few exceptions, 'No'. For anything between these extremes, the answer depends on what you are going to give to music, unless you have some disability that precludes success, such as being completely deaf or tone-deaf.

By beginning this book, you have demonstrated that you have one of the essential ingredients of success, which is that you want to make music.

Using this book

Private teachers of the recorder are rare, and good teachers by definition rarer still, so many recorder players are self-taught. Unfortunately the self-taught player sometimes has to go the long way round to find out important things that a teacher would introduce as a matter of course; so this book has been designed to act as a substitute teacher as far as possible, commenting on all those details which do not appear in the average tutor.

There are of course many recorder tutor-books available, and although it is possible to learn from this book alone, beginners are advised to use a recorder tutor-book (see page 9) as the main source of exercises, referring to this text as difficulties arise and reading it alongside the tutor for necessary extra material. In this way they will have more material for practice than can be printed here, as well as information that is rarely given in tutor-books.

Whatever stage you are at, this is very much a book to keep by you to refer to when difficulties arise. In order to make the 'reference' aspect of the book as useful as possible, the technical exercises and tables of alternative and trill fingerings appear in their own section in the centre of the book where they can be found in a moment. For this reason too, the notes given in Chapter 3 are set out in chromatic sequence rather than in the order in which they are most easily learned.

SECTION 1 deals with preliminaries: what equipment you will need, care of the instrument, and basic fingerings, with comments on various things that have caused difficulties to some of my pupils. For those whose knowledge of the written language of music is insufficient, I have included a chapter on the rudiments of music (Chapter 21), and one on elementary harmony (Chapter 22).

SECTION 2 deals with matters that will arise during the first period of learning, such as tonguing, basic technique, and practice.

SECTION 3 deals with the advanced forms of the material of Section 2, which you will need when you have, for instance, learnt the fingerings and are ready to play with others.

SECTION 4 gives you an extensive chart of basic fingerings, alternative fingerings, and trill fingerings, with a set of technical exercises which you will find useful at all stages of learning.

SECTION 5 deals mainly with matters of interpretation and artistic playing, for those who have a fair knowledge of technique and who are growing in experience.

SECTION 6 deals with a number of matters that will interest the more experienced player, and particularly those who want to play with others.

Throughout this book I have given information for both C recorders (descant and tenor) and F recorders (sopranino, treble and bass) side by side.

The photographs illustrate information about recorders that is better shown in pictures than words.

I should perhaps say that almost every statement about music can be qualified, but if beginners are given the whole picture immediately, they may be overwhelmed by exceptions to and qualifications of the rules. Some of the earlier statements are, therefore, broad general rules which may be qualified later.

STEPHEN F. GOODYEAR

SECTION 1

1 Equipment

There are five sizes of recorder in general use. From the smallest to the largest, they are called sopranino, descant, treble, tenor, and bass (see Plate 1), and the first thing for a beginner to decide is which one he wants to play. No one of them is more difficult to play than any other, since they all use the same patterns of fingerings, but each has its own characteristics. Music of all grades of difficulty is available for all sizes, and the difference in price between the first four sizes, at least, is not great.

Which size or sizes of recorder you will eventually play depends on your temperament and opportunities as much as on anything else, and you can begin on any one of them. Listen to different sizes being played before you make up your mind. If you don't know any recorder players, there are always broadcasts and records to listen to, but be careful that you are not influenced by the player rather than the instrument. If you are lucky, you will soon know what you want to play; if not, try some recorders and see. At the present moment plastic recorders are cheap, and many of them are first-class instruments.

Nobody can tell you which is the best make. There are several brands of plastic recorder which are technically good enough for the concert platform, but players develop their own preferences. Of course different makes have different qualities, but these will not be appreciated by a beginner, and, in the first stages of learning, they don't matter. As you learn to play you will begin to appreciate and to use the individual qualities of your instrument. When you are far enough advanced to play in consort (that is, with other players), it is easier, but not necessarily better, for all members to use the same make; but as a beginner you are going to change your opinions as you learn, and what satisfies you now may not satisfy you in the future. So start with a good cheap instrument. Take advice if you can. Ask your music shop; they know what their customers have found satisfactory, and they want you to come back again. I use a variety of makes myself, and there are always new models appearing.

Avoid cheap second-hand recorders. String instruments may improve with age, but wind instruments do not, particularly when they have keys. Buy a best-selling make and don't be in a hurry to change. Try to have one with an adjustable bottom joint so that you can turn it to suit your own little finger.

There is a benefit in playing recorders that few modern instruments enjoy: if you have learnt the treble, you have also learnt the sopranino (and, once you can read the bass clef, the bass). If you play the descant, you can also play the tenor.

Most recorder-players use more than one instrument, and you will almost certainly end up with more than one size. Conversion from descant to tenor, or from treble to sopranino or bass, is very easy; it is merely a matter of getting used to the different sizes. But to convert from C recorders (descant and tenor) to F recorders (sopranino, treble, and bass) is a little more difficult, because although they all use the same pattern of fingerings, they produce different notes (all fingers down on C recorders gives C, but the same fingering on F recorders gives F). For this reason you should not try to learn C and F recorders simultaneously. Wait until you have a good mastery of one or the other. Nevertheless, aim to learn both types in the end; your opportunities are so much greater.

Each size of recorder has its own characteristics and possibilities. Ranges are given in the Glossary (and see Plate 1).

Sopranino

It is a general rule with wind instruments that the shorter the tube, the higher the note. The sopranino plays the highest notes of the five sizes, and can be so small that some people have difficulty in getting their fingers close enough together. It is a charming instrument to play, and since recorders sound as if they were playing an octave lower than they actually are, it should not make shrill and piercing noises.

The amount of music that *can* be played on the sopranino is enormous, since it includes the whole of the treble repertoire, but there are few sopranino parts in consort music, and not many genuine solos available.

Descant

Most people begin on the descant, and so many instruments are sold that prices are extremely low for the standard of precision involved. There is a large library of music for solo descant and for consorts involving descant parts, but there is less solo descant music than treble, since, as the name implies, it is intended to play above the melody line, and the treble is the true solo instrument.

Treble

Although the treble is twice as long as the sopranino and approximately $1\frac{1}{2}$ times as long as a descant, very few people find it too large, and there is no reason why beginners should not start on the treble. Its tone is beautiful and expressive, and the library of available music, of all periods and kinds, is enormous.

Most consorts have treble parts, and when you reach a reasonable standard, there are trio and quartet sonatas for treble recorders and other instruments which are delightful to play and not exceptionally difficult.

Tenor

The tenor is twice as long as the descant, and players with small hands sometimes have difficulty in covering all the holes. The most common model has one key which is used to cover the bottom hole, and dedicated tenor players with very small hands can obtain a handmade model with several keys. If you are considering a keyless model, make sure that your right little finger can cover the lowest hole with all the other fingers down. It may feel difficult at first, but if your finger *can* cover the hole, you can learn to use it efficiently.

Tenor tone is a little more veiled than that of the treble, and solo music is not always easy to find, though all descant solos *can* be played on the tenor. Most consorts have tenor parts.

Bass

The bass recorder has a charm of its own. Its tone may seem weak, when you first hear it, but one bass recorder will balance a surprisingly large number of other recorders in consort, and the sound of a consort with bass recorder is extremely beautiful.

Solo music is comparatively rare (though again all the treble repertoire is available), but there are many consorts with bass parts. Since bass recorders are (as yet) comparatively expensive, bass players are usually welcome wherever they go.

Other models

In the course of its very long history, the recorder has developed and changed; and there is a great difference in tone (and some difference in fingering) between 'Renaissance' (pre-eighteenth-century) and 'Baroque' (eighteenth-century) recorders. Production in Great Britain and elsewhere has mainly settled on what I shall call the 'standard English' model, which is a development of the eighteenth-century recorder (the 'Baroque' model); you should at least start with one of these. However, 'Renaissance' and other models are available: one can buy descants in D, trebles in G and A, great basses in C, early models and even a 'garklein Flötlein' ('very small flutelet') which can only be played by those with very small hands. But the music for these is limited, and most of them are handmade and correspondingly expensive. If you are interested, your music shop should be able to put you in touch with a specialist shop or maker, and there are now specialist magazines for players of early music. See also pages 152–157.

There is one difference that you should watch for. Some makers, mostly German, attempt to provide what they call a 'more logical' fingering for recorders, partly to avoid complicated fingerings. This makes little difference in playing, provided that you use the correct fingering, but you will play out of tune if you use standard English fingering on a recorder that is not designed for it. Most recorders with non-standard fingering come with a fingering chart in the box; if you compare it with the fingerings given in Chapter 3 you will know whether or not the fingering is standard. Be particularly careful over the descant C^1 sharp, and the treble F^1 sharp.

The parts of the recorder

Plates 2–4 are labelled to make the definitions clearer.

A recorder may have no joints, or one, or more; but the number of joints should make no difference to the performance. Normally one part (the male joint) slips into another (the female joint) and the surfaces in contact usually have a softer lining.

This protects the wood, or any other material from which the instrument is made, from wear and it also seals the joint. Various materials are used for the lining (sometimes called 'lapping'). Plastic is now quite common and does not need greasing, whereas the more traditional cork or thread lappings do.

There are several holes in the tube of the recorder, which may be covered or uncovered by the fingers, and so decide the effective length of the tube in use. Some double finger-holes are used to make certain fingerings easier.

The instrument's tone and performance are governed by the design of the head-joint and other parts (see Plates 3–4). When you move a current of air down the windway, it is shaped and guided on to the knife-edge. Part is deflected outside the instrument and part into the tube, where it sets up vibrations which produce a note of the required pitch and tone.

The opening in the front of the head-joint is sometimes called the 'window'.

Some of the larger recorders—the bass occasionally, the great bass and larger recorders frequently—have a 'spike'; this is a rod which fits into a socket at the bottom of the instrument and supports its weight, while allowing the air to pass out freely.

Material

So far I have assumed that plastic is the best material for your recorder, and in my opinion this is right. Plastic recorders are made in such quantity that the most rigid standards of precision can be used, whereas wood is much less suitable for mass-production, since no two pieces of wood are exactly alike.

Of course, if you want the best available, then you must buy a handmade wooden instrument from a really good maker; but such a recorder could cost thirty to forty times as much as its plastic equivalent, and most makers have a long waiting-list. There is no doubt that the craftsman-made instrument should be better than the mass-produced plastic, but in actual fact the difference is minimal, and can only be detected by the trained ear.

If you do order a good wooden instrument, make sure that you have the thumb-hole 'bushed' (i.e. lined with a harder material) so that it does not wear under the pressure of your thumb-nail. As for choice of wood, there is no doubt that different woods produce different qualities of tone, but it is also true that two recorders made from the same piece of wood can vary in tone. Take the maker's advice if possible, but also try, if you can, a recorder made from the same type of wood as the instrument you are considering.

Other equipment

With your recorder you should have one or two other things, of which the most important is some sort of mop to dry out the instrument after playing. Germs and moulds flourish in a warm damp environment, and the moisture inside the instrument can collect dust and build up deposits which can alter the playing characteristics of the instrument.

Remember that transferring the moisture to a mop and leaving the mop in your recorder case will not get rid of possible germs, and a dirty mop may leave dirt where it is not wanted. The best cleaning tool is a stick with an eye in the end to which you can attach replaceable pieces of rag.

If you do use one of these, make sure that the rag and stick are not over-tight inside the recorder, since it has a tapering tube and could split. Always fold the rag over the end of the stick when cleaning the head-joint and go gently—you could move the fipple-block or damage the knife-edge (see Chapter 2 and plates 2 and 4).

A case is useful but not essential; the box your recorder came in will stand wear for quite a time. Some players obtain a small case with a lid, fill it with a block of plastic foam, and cut out shaped beds for their instruments and equipment. If you look at what other players use, you will eventually know what you want and be able to buy it or make it for yourself.

Stands

Music stands are necessary. If you lay the music on a table you will find that your head has to droop to read the music, and this hampers your breathing and breath control. At the very least your music must be propped up, and you cannot always expect to find a convenient surface for this.

You need a durable stand which has a desk of reasonable size, and which will fold to something which you can carry without too much difficulty. Again, don't be in a hurry to buy until you have seen other people's stands; there are many models.

Tone-projection

Messrs. Dolmetsch (see page 152) make what they call a tone-projector, which is a wheelbarrow-shaped plastic apparatus to be fastened (with a rubber band) to the head-joint. It does amplify the sound, to some extent, and you may find one or two of them (they come in two sizes) useful for performance.

Recorder tutors

You should choose a tutor to accompany this book, and a number of tutors are available in most countries of the world. In general terms, you need one which is clear in its instruction and which contains as much musical material (i.e. exercises and tunes) as possible. You will perhaps forgive me if I confess to a preference for my own publications.

Thumb-rests

Some recorders are sold with thumb-rests (also called thumb-hooks) for the right thumb; and there is no doubt that they are a convenience for most players. With plastic recorders, you can shape a piece of cork, wood, or plastic, and stick it on the recorder (just *above* your right thumb) and with wooden recorders you can also buy metal fittings that can be screwed or stuck on. Screwing on is better done by skilled hands. If someone else is doing it for you, make sure that you mark exactly where you want the fitting to be put.

2   The Care of Your Recorder

The greatest risk to a recorder is of being sat or stood on. Never, for example, leave a recorder on a chair. When you are not playing it, put it away in its case, and make sure that the case is in a safe place.

First, and most important, always remove any moisture after playing, taking care to avoid damaging your recorder. Your cleaning rod should be of softer material than your instrument.

Cork-lined joints benefit from an occasional greasing. Use standard joint-grease, or vaseline, and don't put too much on. When you have greased the joint and re-assembled it, wipe away the grease from the exterior.

Occasionally you can brighten up the varnish and clean it with almond oil and a soft cloth. Use little oil and much rubbing.

From time to time you should make sure that the windway and finger-holes are clean (see *Obstructions* below).

Obstructions

The stream of air that passes through a recorder while it is being played carries dust, which can build up in certain parts and affect the tone and the intonation. Also, loose objects can get into the bore while it is in its case. So the bore and the windway should be cleaned regularly.

The greatest care must be taken to avoid damage to the knife-edge, because the instrument's performance depends on this remaining clean and sharp. A feather will normally be enough to clean out the windway, but it will not clean the corners very well, and occasionally you should use a piece of card (though never anything stronger). If you have any obstructions that you can't deal with, go to an instrument repairer.

If you decide to deal with the trouble yourself, start by taking out the fipple-block. First make sure that the block is removable, then take a short length of dowel (round wooden rod), a little smaller in diameter than the width of the bore; slide it in, hold the head-joint, and tap the dowel gently on a suitable surface. Then clean out the corners of the windway, both on the block and inside the head, and slide the fipple-block back in, until it is exactly in place. Do not remove fipple-blocks unless you have to; with some types of recorders it is possible to force them back wrongly and do damage.

Obstructions elsewhere are usually easily removed if you remember that the recorder has a tapering bore and work with the taper, not against it.

Moisture

The most frequent form of trouble comes from moisture condensed from your breath, particularly when the recorder is cold. Some condensation is inevitable, and there is a school of thought which believes that the recorder produces its best tone when there is a light film of moisture in the bore; but excessive moisture will affect the tone or intonation, even to the point of silencing some notes.

The most usual places for moisture to collect and affect playing are in and around the 'window', on the knife-edge, or at the bottom of the windway. This can easily be removed by a short, sharp blow into the windway or into the window. You can manage this quietly if you cover the window with a finger.

A wooden recorder, particularly, can be so seriously affected by extra moisture that it should not be played, and must be put away to dry slowly. When wood is moistened, it tends to swell, and even though most manufacturers impregnate the wood, swelling can still occur, and can lead to splitting (though this is more often due to over-rapid drying) and to stiff joints.

Joints

In all recorders, the walls of the male joint are thinner than those of the bore, and so joints are weak places. A mop with a wire handle can cause damage, and so can careless handling. Whenever you separate a joint, do it with a gentle rotary action, and make sure that you are not putting strain across the length of the instrument.

When joints become stiff, this danger is increased. If the stiffness is due to moisture, put the recorder away where it can dry slowly, preferably upright with a peg inserted in the foot-joint, away from direct sunshine and any source of heat.

Stiff cork joints can often be eased by a light application of grease, and thread-bound joints by the removal of some thread. Plastic joints are more difficult, but it is rare for them to become stiff. Do not remove thickness from joint-linings by rubbing them down unless it is absolutely necessary.

Should the joints become loose, a strip of thin paper will work for a time (but beware that you do not have an excess which obstructs the bore). With thread joints, you can add more thread, sticking it down with joint-grease, until it becomes necessary to re-wind the whole joint. If you have to do this, you must make the joint fit closely over its whole length, and this needs special care in winding the thread into the correct cylindrical or slightly barrel-shaped form.

Loose cork joints can be temporarily improved by a layer of grease, or by being lightly roughened with sandpaper; but sooner or later they will have to be re-lined. You can do this yourself if you are good with your hands. First clear away the old cork and glue, then cut a strip of cork to size and glue it in the right place, taking care to fit the edges well together. Then sand the cork down to size, if necessary, and grease.

In all cases repairs have to be neat; there must be no bits of cork or ends of thread which will prevent the joint from closing properly. Emergency repairs can sometimes be made with one of the thicker types of sticky tape, such as carpet-edging. Try to find one that is thick enough to need only one layer; the more thicknesses that you have to use, the more temporary will be the repair.

Cracks

If the instrument cracks, you should go to a repairer, because the edges of the crack have to be forced back exactly together, and you are unlikely to have anything that will hold a tapering shape correctly. But if you *have* to repair the crack yourself, a tight whipping with strong cord will often hold the edges together fairly well. Clean out any loose material from the crack and use a good space-filling glue (contact adhesives are not suitable); work the glue well into the crack, bind it tightly, and leave it to dry for the correct period. Then clean away any beads of glue from the outside and inside. Be sure that you use the right type of glue for the material. I have often successfully mended complete breaks on plastic recorders—modern adhesives are remarkably efficient. But the drying must take place under pressure.

Faulty intonation

You cannot deal with this yourself, unless it is due to something simple, such as a bead of moisture in a finger-hole. Check the recorder for obvious faults, look at the fingering-chart in case a non-standard fingering is required, ask another player to test the doubtful notes, and then either send it back to the manufacturer or to an instrument repairer. On no account attempt to alter the size of a finger-hole; this is a real expert's job, since changing the size of one hole may affect several notes.

Oiling

Most wooden recorders need oiling in order to build up a smooth, water-resistant inside coating. When you buy a new wooden recorder, look inside to see whether the bore appears dry and rough. If it does, take a mop of the correct size, put some oil on it, and swab out the bore, taking care that the bore is evenly covered, and that you use the minimum amount of oil. Then leave the instrument to dry for a few days.

Among the oils in general use are almond, linseed, and banana oils. Linseed takes the longest to dry.

Be careful with overflows. When treating the bore it is impossible to prevent the oil getting into the fingerholes, where it can then dry into a coating round the edges, altering the size and shape of the holes. Wipe them out with a matchstick and rag, being particularly careful over the smallest holes. Also remove excess oil from the knife-edge, and clean out the windway.

Keys

Most tenor and bass recorders have keys, and keys tend to go wrong in various provoking ways. All keys have springs; these can break, slip out of their mounting, become soft, and even fall out and get lost. If you are good enough with your hands, you can repair them; if not, take them to a competent repairer. If there is no specialist repairer in your area, a working watchmaker can sometimes be persuaded to do the job. Use rubber bands for emergency repairs.

The pads in keys are intended to seal the holes as your fingers do. They must be made of the right grade of leather, and they have to be in precisely the right position. They tend to harden with age, which is not necessarily a bad thing as they usually harden into the right shape to seal the hole. When oiling, try to keep the oil off pads.

If the pads are faulty, the simplest thing is usually to replace the pad. You can buy pads from music shops, though you usually have to buy a set to get the one you want. It is best to have the job done by an instrument repairer, but if you have to do the job yourself, first remove the pad and clear away any glue from the socket, then stick the new pad in. You will find it easier to remove the key first: the axle usually has a pin through it, which may just slide or be screw-threaded. But you must make sure that the pad is in the correct position and is sealing the hole before the glue hardens.

A broken key cannot always be replaced; manufacturers sometimes change their models and do not keep replacement parts for older ones. So save the pieces until you are sure that you can get a replacement.

A key that sticks may be due to a bent axle, or it may be that you have been careless with your oiling and stuck the pad to its seat. You can sometimes replace an axle with a dressmaker's pin—they come in different sizes.

3 Basic Fingerings

This chapter gives complete note fingerings together with some suggestions which should help you to learn the notes. The notes are presented in chromatic order from the lowest C (descant), F (treble), to make reference as easy as possible. However, when learning notes for the first time, there is an order which makes the learning easier and this is set out below. The musical example (Fig. 1) refers to descant notes only but the treble equivalents are written out below and can easily be found on the following pages.

Descant: B, A, G, D¹, C¹, F♯, D, E, C, F, B♭, C¹♯, E¹, G♯, G¹, F¹, A¹, E¹♭, F¹♯, C♯, E♭, G¹♯, B¹, B¹♭, C¹¹, D¹¹

Treble: E, D¹, C¹, G¹, F¹, B, G, A, F, A♯, D¹♯, F¹♯, A¹, C¹♯, C¹, B¹, D¹, G¹♯, B♭¹, F♯, G♯, C¹♯, E¹, D¹♯, F¹¹, G¹¹

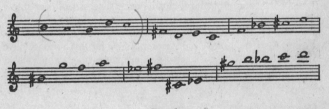

Fig. 1

In Chapter 12 these fingerings are also given in tablature, together with alternative fingerings and trill fingerings.

Figs. 31 and 32 show two useful exercises which will help you to learn new notes.

You should also use the technical exercises in Chapter 13 in conjunction with this chapter, as you will find the initial exercises helpful in learning new notes and difficult note changes. An exercise written for any one note or combination of notes can, of course, be adapted to apply to other notes and combinations.

There is no standard system of numbering fingers. In this book I shall use the following notation:

Left thumb	0	Right first	4
Left first	1	Right middle	5
Left middle	2	Right ring	6
Left ring	3	Right little	7

—except where, in the fingering charts, I use a form of tablature which is self-explanatory. Fingers not mentioned do not cover holes. Each finger has its own hole, and never covers any other.

Where a finger (or thumb) is required to half-cover a hole, a diagonal line is drawn through the figure, thus:

∅   ∮

Where there are dashes by the notes, the dash means 'higher'. Thus C is the lowest note on the descant recorder, C' is one octave higher, and C'' another octave higher.

Cross-fingerings

If recorders were fingered logically, each successive finger taken off above the lowest note would give us the next note above; but there are twelve notes in an octave and we do not have enough fingers. Also, the holes would be impossibly far apart; so we have to use 'abnormal' fingerings to produce some notes which have, as it were, gaps in the pattern, such as 01346 or 0123467. These are called 'cross-fingerings'.

Descant C, Treble F. Fingered 01234567

Fig. 2

With all notes on the recorder, but particularly with lower notes, the greater the breath-pressure, the sharper the note, and vice-versa. If you use the same breath-pressure for lower notes as you use for higher ones, the lower notes will be sharp. With this note, and particularly up to E (descant), A (treble), listen very carefully for faulty intonation.

You may find this note a little difficult to play at first. First check your breath-pressure—it should be very low—and then your fingers. Quite often with beginners the left-hand fingers tend to slip off their holes when the right fingers are being used. Make sure that you have a firm G (descant), C (treble) and then add fingers 4 and 5, 6, and then 7, when you are first learning the note. If your recorder has an adjustable bottom joint, experiment with various positions until your right little finger closes the hole easily.

Descant C sharp/D flat, Treble F sharp/G flat. Fingered 01234567

Fig. 3

This note requires the lowest hole to be half-covered, and your recorder may have a pair of holes instead of one to make this easier. Play C (descant), F (treble) and draw your little finger back until C sharp (descant), F sharp (treble) comes. Continue doing this until you can do it easily, then try going directly to the note.

Descant D, Treble G. Fingered 0123456

Fig. 4

You should have little trouble here, except that in the early stages, some of your fingers may not be cleanly on their holes. Some tenor players may have to learn to stretch their right fingers.

Descant D sharp/E flat, Treble G sharp/A flat. Fingered 0123456̷

Fig. 5

This note, like descant C sharp, requires half-holing, but with finger 6. The same principles apply.

Descant E, Treble A. Fingered 012345

Fig. 6

You should have no difficulty here, though changes to and from descant F sharp, treble B may cause some difficulty later.

Descant F, Treble A sharp/B flat. Fingered 0123467

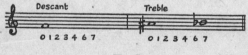

Fig. 7

This is one of the more difficult cross-fingerings. When learning the note, it may help to think of the finger that is up rather than of the fingers that are down.

The most difficult change involving this note is to and from descant E, treble A, and this should be practised regularly.

Descant F sharp/G flat, Treble B. Fingered 012356

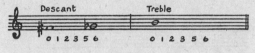

Fig. 8

There may be a little temporary difficulty here, since this is a cross-fingering. Changes to and from descant E, treble A should be practised.

Descant G, Treble C. Fingered 0123

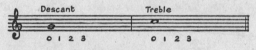

Fig. 9

In the early stages the left first finger may tend to slip off its hole, but this should be solved very quickly.

Descant G sharp/A flat, Treble C sharp/D flat. Fingered 01245

Fig. 10

There are some changes to and from this note that can cause difficulty. Practise particularly the change in Figure 11 (overleaf),

Fig. 11

Descant A, Treble D. Fingered 012

Fig. 12

One of the easiest notes to learn.

Descant A sharp/B flat, Treble D sharp/E flat. Fingered 01346

Fig. 13

One of the more important notes to learn well. Practise particularly changes to and from A descant, D treble.

Descant B, Treble E. Fingered 01

Fig. 14

The easiest note of all, and probably the first note that you will learn.

Descant C¹, Treble F¹. Fingered 02

Fig. 15

There may be momentary difficulty, but it will soon be learnt. Practise particularly changes to and from descant B, treble E. There is an alternative fingering for descant B, treble E which makes such changes easier, but master the normal fingering first (see Chapters 12 and 13).

Descant C¹ sharp/D¹ flat, Treble F¹ sharp/G¹ flat. Fingered 12

Fig. 16

If your right thumb is in playing position you will have no difficulty in supporting the recorder, even with your left thumb off. Some recorders, usually German, require another fingering for this note, usually 0. See pages 21 and 56.

Descant D¹ Treble G¹. Fingered 2

Fig. 17

Keep your right thumb in playing position and you should have no difficulty in holding the recorder; but don't use any other means of support.

Descant D¹ sharp/E flat, Treble G¹ sharp/A¹ flat. Fingered 23456, sometimes 123456

Fig. 18

This is one of the least satisfactory notes on the recorder, often having poor tone and excess volume. Nevertheless it is important, and must be well learnt.

Descant E¹, Treble A¹. Fingered Ø12345

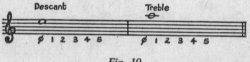

Fig. 19

With this note, as with most notes of the upper register, the thumb-hole should be partly open. In general, and for most makes of recorder, this opening should be as small as possible, and the only way of ensuring this is to bend the thumb and snap the thumb-nail into the hole. This is accurate and quick, and the amount of hole left open can be regulated by bending the thumb. Some authorities recommend starting with the minimum amount of hole uncovered, and then bending the thumb further to increase the opening. A long thumb-nail makes this technique very difficult. I keep my thumb-nail as short as reasonably possible, particularly on the left-hand side.

With this note, and one or two others, the octave jump may be made by increasing the breath-pressure and tonguing a little more vigorously. Although this can be useful at times, it should be used as little as possible.

Descant F¹, Treble A¹ sharp/B¹ flat. Fingered Ø12346

Fig. 20

As this fingering so much resembles that of the lower octave, it will be quickly learnt, but notice that finger 7 should not remain down for the upper note. In quick passages it is permissible to use the upper fingering Ø12346 for upper and lower notes, but this gives a slightly sharp lower F, unless care is taken to reduce breath-pressure.

Descant F¹ sharp/G¹ flat, Treble B¹. Fingered Ø1235

Fig. 21

There should be no trouble here, though I have known some people to confuse this fingering with that for descant G¹ sharp, treble C¹ sharp.

Descant G¹, Treble C¹. Fingered Ø123

Fig. 22

This has the same fingering as descant G, treble C, except for the partly open thumb-hole.

Descant G¹ sharp/A¹ flat, Treble C¹ sharp/D¹ flat. Fingered Ø124

Fig. 23

Again, little trouble should be expected. If there is difficulty in remembering the fingering, think of A¹ being lowered by the right-hand finger.

Descant A¹, Treble D¹. Fingered Ø12

Fig. 24

A very easy fingering to learn. With these higher notes, be careful not to make the tone harsh by overblowing.

Descant A¹ sharp/B¹ flat, Treble D¹ sharp/E¹ flat. Fingered Ø1256

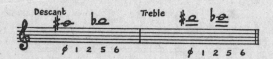

Fig. 25

This fingering is sometimes confused with the next semitone higher in the early stages. Apart from this, there should be no trouble.

Descant B^I, Treble E^I. Fingered Ø1245

Fig. 26

This is no more difficult than the preceding note.

Descant C^{II}, Treble F^{II}. Fingered Ø145

Fig. 27

There is little difficulty over learning the fingering, but the tone of this note, and of the highest notes in general, may require some practice. Try a crisp tonguing to start the note, and use as little breath as possible, so that there is no sense of strain about the tone. In the past I have found some cheaper recorders which would not play this note, but nowadays this is rare.

Descant C^{II} sharp/D^{II} flat, Treble F^{II} sharp/G^{II} flat
This is probably the most difficult note on the recorder, so much so that there is no standard fingering for it, and at least one maker makes a special key for it. However, it does occur occasionally, though more often for treble players. Look at the alternative fingerings in Chapter 12 and try to find one that suits you and your recorder.

Descant D^{II}, Treble G^{II}. Fingered Ø1346

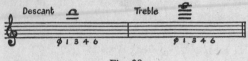

Fig. 28

This note is no more difficult to produce than descant C[II], treble F[II], and occurs occasionally.

Descant G[II], Treble C[II]. Fingered Ø14

Fig. 29

This note occurs very occasionally, more often for treble players. The fingering produces no difficulty, but often the tone needs practice.

Other notes

It is possible to produce the notes between D[II] and G[II] (descant), G[II] and C[II] (treble), but I have never seen them used. Fingerings can be found in Chapter 12, if they are desired.

SECTION 2

4 Basic Technique

This chapter is an introduction to basic technique for beginners and will help you tackle the first stages of learning the recorder. Some of the points covered (tonguing, the use of the breath and practice) are explained in more depth in the later chapters in this section.

Much of the job of learning a musical instrument consists of forming as many correct habits as possible. It is difficult to avoid getting into some bad habits—there are so many different things about which you should be informed that if you were exposed to all of them at once you would never get started; but the advice that follows will show you which are bad habits and which are good.

Playing position

You are going to want to be able to control your breath pressure very exactly, to be able to breathe gently into the recorder for quite long periods, and to be able to take in controlled amounts of breath very quickly. So, within reason, your position should be one that makes these things easy. Your head should be upright, so that your throat is not constricted. Your body should also be upright enough to allow you to use your lungs and diaphragm freely, without being rigid or tense. Also, you must be able to see the music and the other players, when there are any. Equally, you must not feel uncomfortable or you will not be able to play properly. However, you should also realise that what may feel uncomfortable now, when you are beginning, need not feel uncomfortable when you have established correct habits.

If you play standing—and you should, from time to time—see that your weight is evenly distributed on both feet, and that you are at ease and not tense when you play.

Make sure that you can see your music and still maintain a

good position, remembering always that you must be able to see over the top of the stand.

The hands

As far as possible, your fingers should be at right angles to the recorder, and straight without being rigid; and you should close the holes with the pads, not the tips, of your fingers (see Plate 5). The larger the recorder you play, the less easy this is, particularly for the right hand, and a modified position is normally used. In this the right hand is kept with the fingers as nearly at right angles to the recorder as possible, but size of hands and suppleness of fingers may require the fingers to point downwards to some extent.

Your right hand should always be in playing position. Fingers which are not stopping holes should be above them. They should not be far away but remember that if you have them too close, they will affect intonation.

Provided that your recorder has an adjustable bottom joint, it does not matter whether your right hand or your left is nearer to your mouth; at all periods of history, players have used either position. But there are good reasons for the normal position, with the left hand nearer your mouth, one of which is that not all recorders have an adjustable bottom joint. Also, if you ever go on to another wind instrument, reversed hands will not be possible. If you are strongly right-handed, it is a mistake to keep the right hand at the top. Both hands have to acquire equal facility, and by beginning with your better hand you are only postponing the problem of using the other.

With some fingerings, such as D^1 (descant), G^1 (treble) it is permissible to use another finger for support, and there is a school of 'buttress-fingering' which allows for this; but as far as possible, use standard fingering and, if you need to support the instrument, make sure that any fingers you put down do not affect the intonation. Your recorder can be held quite securely between your lips, your left middle finger, and your right thumb.

Some beginners develop the habit of looking at the instrument to see whether their fingers are correctly placed. This is always bad. Your eyes should be on the music, and you should check the correctness of your fingering by touch and by ear. If the sound is wrong, you are doing something wrong; but look at the recorder only when you have taken it away from your mouth, and then only if it is really necessary.

You will soon discover that your fingers are not fully independent; when you move one, then others move too, particularly when you move your little or ring finger. This is quite normal, and you will improve as you learn to play. As long as the involuntary movement does not cause intonation to be affected, it does not matter unless it makes some cross-fingerings impossible, or unless it worries you.

There are some exercises you can do to help the independence of your fingers. They are all based on moving one or more fingers while keeping the others still. You can move each finger separately, or move fingers in pairs; 1 and 2, 3 and 4; 1 and 3, 2 and 4, and so on.

(1) Rest the tips of your fingers on any convenient surface and tap, singly and in combinations.
(2) Keep all your fingers straight, then bend either each finger in turn, or pairs of fingers in combinations.
(3) Bend your fingers until the pads touch the bases; brace the fingers back until the first joints are in line with the back of the hand, then move the knuckles singly and in combinations.

Breath pressure

The recorder should never be held between the teeth; the lips should cushion it and seal round it. Some authorities recommend drawing the lips back over the teeth, as in oboe-playing; but as far as I can see, this does not affect the tone and makes sealing more difficult.

If you want to produce a clean, consistent note, then you have to produce a controlled and level breath-pressure. If your breath-pressure varies, then so will the pitch and volume of the note, unless the variation is very small. This effect can be used, but it must be under control and in the early stages you should aim to produce notes of level pitch and volume.

Taking breath

Breathing in takes time, and there will not always be a convenient rest in which you can breathe. Open your mouth and breathe in as quickly as possible, taking care not to take in too much air. As a general rule, you will hardly ever have to more than half-fill your lungs.

You must not, of course, breathe in in the wrong places. Most music has breath-marks, which indicate where a break must be made; and they are usually spaced so that you can breathe conveniently. For further information see Chapters 6, 10 and 14.

Tonguing

When you tongue a note, you use the tongue as a valve for the column of air you are producing. Tonguing is essential; the only time you should not tongue a note is during a slur, when the first note should be tongued and the rest follow without a break. Untongued notes, apart from slurring, sound very bad.

Begin every tongued note with a movement of the tongue as if you were saying 'T'. Not '*Tee*', or '*Tur*'—just the sound of the letter T. End every note in the same way. When you are doing this correctly, every note should come out as a solid bar of sound. Remember that the note should end as cleanly as it began and above all, avoid letting the ends of the notes droop away into a lower pitch.

If your tutor uses some other letter than 'T', then either follow the tutor or use 'T'. See Chapters 5 and 9 for further material about tonguing.

Accurate playing

Make sure that you are really doing what is required of you. A written note or rest is a measure of duration, so if you are playing the notes in the correct places, but only playing each note for a short time, you are not only playing the music incorrectly, but also building up bad habits. Your playing *must* be correct in practice. Sight-reading is another matter, and different rules apply; but in practice you must aim at absolute precision, even if it means going slowly for a while. Fig. 30 illustrates the common fault of failing to give notes their full value.

Fig. 30

The use of memory

You have a certain amount to memorise, even if you are not new
to music, and no doubt you would like to learn with the minimum
amount of effort. There is a theory that we remember everything,
but suppress unwanted memories and build pathways to the
memories we need. These pathways can be reinforced by repetition, variety of approach, and in many other ways. Therefore,
when you have something new to learn, use your new facts in as
many ways as possible; play exercises, read them, sing them,
copy them out and, in particular, try to find the reasons for them
and relate them to what you already know. For instance, if you
have F sharp (descant) to learn, and already know G,A,B,C, and
D, play the exercise in Fig. 31 and then compose for yourself a
more complicated version, perhaps like Fig. 32. Write it down,
sing it and play it.

Fig. 31

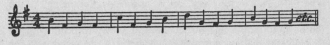

Fig. 32

Difficult passages

Some changes between notes are easier than others. For example, it is always easier to change from B to A (descant), E to D (treble), than it is from B flat to A (descant), E flat to D (treble); in many difficult passages, the trouble can be traced to one difficult change between two notes. Therefore, when you have trouble with a passage, analyse it to find where the difficulty lies, and practise that part only. Then put it back into context and see whether you have improved.

When you are practising a change, you must not practise errors into it. Take it slowly and make sure that you do it correctly. Play your first note for as long as is necessary while you mentally rehearse what you are going to do; then make the change as quickly as possible; then repeat, making as sure as possible that you are correct each time.

It is very important that your practice should contain as few errors as possible. Practise slowly, so slowly that you can avoid making mistakes; then speed up gradually until you do make a mistake; then go more slowly to cure that mistake, and so on. Fast playing as a diagnostic exercise can be useful, but you will not cure errors by playing a piece too fast and hoping that it will come right in the end. If you are going to perform, you should be able to play a piece faster than you will actually play it at the performance; it gives you a feeling of security which is invaluable.

The beat

It is very important to practise to a regular beat; this will help you to avoid the common habit of skating over difficult passages so that you can appear to be playing fast. However, playing to a regular beat is very difficult to do without some help.

A piece of string with a weight at one end will give you a regular beat, but a metronome is more useful. It will not only set a regular beat for you at any speed that you are likely to need; it can also ring a bell every 2, 3, 4, or 6 beats. Set the bell to the correct number of beats, and play in such a way that it rings at the beginning of each bar. Set the beat slowly to begin with, so as to avoid making mistakes, then increase the speed, slowing down and correcting mistakes when you make them.

Speed of finger-movement

Music has a great influence on us; where the music that we play is slow, we tend to make slow movements. But in finger-movements there is only one speed—the fastest possible. For example, when you play B to A (descant), E to D (treble), slurred, the pitch of the upper note tends to slide downwards as finger 2 approaches its hole. This will always happen, no matter how fast the finger moves, but the slide can be made imperceptible by speed of movement. In unslurred playing the finger moves during the gap between tonguings; but if the tonguings and finger movement do not coincide, the effect can be blurred.

Physical difficulties

If you find that you have any particular troubles, practice with special emphasis on them ought to help; if it does not, you will either have to take professional advice or reorganise your playing so that you can handle your difficulties. Some people have learnt to overcome the greatest difficulties in playing an instrument. Django Reinhardt, the guitarist, had two almost useless fingers on his left hand, and there have been many blind players.

5 Tonguing *(Beginners)*

The purposes of tonguing are (*a*) to give shape to notes and phrases; (*b*) to mark out groups of notes (i.e. to articulate the music); (*c*) to make playing easier (sometimes); and (*d*) to add interest and variety to a performance.

There are many kinds of tonguing—I have found over a hundred and twenty—but the essence of the matter can be put fairly simply. In order to shape a note well, the tongue is used as a valve for the current of air; and this is done by shaping a consonant with the tongue to begin the note, usually 'T' or 'D'. The same motion is used to end a note cleanly.

Different consonants need different movements of the tongue, and so affect the character of the note; 'T' is crisper and lighter, 'D' softer and heavier. There are other consonants which can be used, but this is a matter for advanced players (see Chapter 9).

As a beginner you should use 'T' exclusively; later on you can experiment with 'D' and study the different effects that you can produce with these two letters. Your aim should be to find out the maximum speed at which you can single-tongue (use 'T'), and the maximum speed at which you can co-ordinate your fingers and your tongue. This is important, because obviously you cannot play faster than you can tongue (apart from slurred passages), and because you cannot keep up fast single-tonguing for long.

Just how fast you can manage single-tonguing is affected as much as anything by the way you speak. If your local accent or language is soft and warm, you may have what is called a 'lazy tongue'; if your speech is brisk and well-articulated, then you may have better control of your tongue. If you have pursued a course of elocution lessons, or have acted regularly, your tongue may be able to move more quickly.

Exercises

You can improve your control of your tongue by repetition of
the basis consonants 'T' and 'D', or, to add interest, by using
tongue-twisters. The most useful are those which mainly concern
the letters T, D, G, H, K, L, and R. You should endeavour to
make your consonants as light and clean as possible, and to increase your speed.

Double-tonguing

When you have a good mastery of single-tonguing, you can start
to explore double-tonguing, which allows you to play faster.
This is dealt with more thoroughly in Chapter 9, but you can
begin to use it quite early in your musical life.

For your present purposes, 'T–K–' or 'D–G–' will suffice. You
gain speed by using, as it were, both ends of your tongue.

However, this does not mean that you will instantly gain speed
by using these new tonguings. Much depends on your control of
the muscles involved, and you may well find that double-tonguing
is slower at first than single-tonguing; in this case it is essential
to practise double-tonguing thoroughly until it is faster than
single-tonguing. Aim for evenness and lightness.

Slurring and tonguing

Slurring and tonguing are used to add variety, beauty and interest
to music. There are many possible combinations of slurring and
tonguing, but the following figures illustrate four standard
patterns:

Fig. 33

Fig. 34

Fig. 35

Fig. 36

Each of these patterns produces a different effect. Look through your music from time to time and practise it with different combinations of slurring and tonguing. Listen very carefully to the effect, so that in time you will be able to decide on the best way to slur and tongue a passage where the slurs are not given. Also, practise as many regular patterns of slurring and tonguing as you can find. The greater your mastery of all the details of technique, the more your mind will be free to concentrate on interpretation.

6   The Use of the Breath *(Beginners)*

Breath control

Before you can learn to use your breath well, you must get the processes of breathing (inhalation and exhalation) under control. Breathing is semi-automatic, but playing wind instruments requires really controlled breathing.

What your limits are at this moment is for you to discover, but whatever they are, you can improve with training and with practice. Playing will improve your breath-control, provided that you listen to yourself and try to improve, but progress will be more rapid under guidance.

The sound of your instrument is produced and modified by the way in which you breathe into it. In most wind instruments the placing of the lips affects the sound, but this is only true of the recorder in that your lips must seal round the mouthpiece and leave the opening of the windway clear. The tone and intonation are dependent on the speed and character of the column of air that passes through the windway, and these depend on control of your body.

The column of air needs to be steady and of the right speed. If you finger any note and put air through the instrument in varying quantities and at different speeds, you will produce a sound that varies in volume and pitch. If you overdo the quantity of air or its speed, you may 'crack' the note. Within fairly close limits you can get a variation of volume without discernible variation of pitch, and you should practise doing this until you know the limits of volume-change you can manage.

Vibrato

It is probable that when you play a long note you will produce variations in volume (and perhaps pitch) by lack of control. This effect is called vibrato.

Vibrato is caused by varying breath-pressure, and should be controlled from the diaphragm. The exercise given in Chapter 10 (Breathing) will help you to control your natural vibrato, but you must listen to yourself, and learn to play with or without vibrato as required, and to control the extent and speed of the vibrato.

This control is important, since recorder-players should not always use vibrato. Indeed, there are many people who say that vibrato should never be used, except as a special effect, and then only in music of certain periods. I would not entirely agree with this, but there is no doubt that you must learn both to control your vibrato and to play without it.

Watch any orchestra and you will see vibrato being used. The string players rock their left hands to and fro to produce it, and they would consider any music dull without vibrato. Watch also the extent and speed of the string-players' movements; Italian string-players often use a slow, wide vibrato, whereas British vibrato often approaches a mere nervous snatch.

To control your vibrato is more difficult than it sounds, but it can be done. Yoga breathing exercises, or some singing exercises can help, but most of all, listen carefully to yourself and try to produce the sound you want. If you have a good tape recorder, it helps to record yourself playing long notes and to listen to your mistakes. Make sure that your machine is sufficiently accurate for this purpose (see Chapter 7, *correcting mistakes*).

Breathing and breath-marks

When and where you take breath is most important. Much of the effect of music depends on its being punctuated correctly, so much so that breath-marks are given in most recorder music and should be followed. The term 'to take breath' does not always mean an actual intake of air; it is sometimes sufficient or necessary for the tongue to make the punctuation, and you may have to use the same breath over quite a long phrase, punctuating it by tonguing. I would suggest that a normal person could sustain a passage of notes in one breath for about thirty seconds without discomfort—after they have learnt the requisite control.

The first essential is not to take in more breath than you can handle, nor less than is needed, and this you will learn through experience. Always look ahead in the score and estimate how much breath you will need. If you do find yourself short of breath near the end of a phrase, you can always squeeze out a few more notes by using your diaphragm. The sensation is something like tightening your stomach muscles. Any good singing tutor will give you exercises to improve your lung-capacity and to extend your control.

Secondly, make sure that you are not losing air by not sealing your lips round the mouthpiece.

Thirdly, practise deep-breathing and letting out the air in a controlled way. If you have taken in too much air, you can let some of the surplus out through your nose, even while playing; but it is sometimes difficult to avoid letting out too much.

Phrasing

Apart from breath-marks, the music itself will tell you where you can take breath, once you can recognise the correct places (see Chapter 14). For the moment you can use the following rules.

(1) Where there are breath-marks in the music, they must be observed.
(2) You can always take breath at rests.
(3) Where necessary you can take breath at the end of long notes, by clipping their lengths slightly; but you *must* play the next note at the correct time, and you must make the clipping as short as you can.
(4) Where you have to play a note after a rest or breath mark, you must breathe in before the note should begin; don't fall into the common error of *preparing* to play a note when you should be playing it.

You should make every effort to understand phrasing, because it makes such a difference to the music. Provided that you are alert and responsive, there is something to be learnt from every piece of music that you hear or play. Try the effect of phrasing one of your pieces differently, remembering that two players may disagree over phrasing and that there is room for more than one interpretation. Of course, some opinions are better than others but there is no definitive performance of any piece of music. You should also discuss your ideas with other people; there is always something to be learnt, particularly when you can arrive at the reasons for differences of opinion.

7 Practice *(Beginners)*

Practice is the only way for you to improve and it is worth making sure your practice is as efficient as possible, so that you learn the greatest amount possible with the minimum effort. In order to do this, you must know what you are trying to do, and you must use your time fully. Your practice periods should be planned so that you can give concentrated attention to all the things that need improvement.

In the early stages, most of your time must be spent on basic technique; learning all the notes, learning to read music fluently, improving breath- and finger-control, and the beginnings of interpretation.

Remember that time spent on playing things through for pleasure, without attempting to improve, is not practice, though it can be used for noting things that need attention.

Duration of practice

There is no one length of time which is appropriate for all individuals. A professional player may spend eight hours or so in practice every day; a beginner certainly will not be able to work that long profitably. Ideally, a practice period should last as long as improvement is being made, and should stop as soon as the player is only teaching himself to make mistakes.

Regular practice is important. Ten minutes each day, properly planned and used, is of much more benefit than four hours once a week.

Correcting mistakes

If you make the same mistake twice, you are beginning to teach yourself the wrong thing: all practice should be done at so slow a speed that no mistakes are made. Fast playing should only be used to discover the parts that need attention.

The most important reason for attempting to get rid of mistakes is to free your mind for interpretation of the music. The basic method of eliminating mistakes (though not the only one) is to identify the cause of the mistake and to repeat the correct version. You should begin by playing so slowly that you don't make mistakes, then increase your speed until mistakes start to occur and then analyse and correct each mistake. Keep a constant speed when you practise—don't slow down over difficult passages; and never begin a piece or an exercise so fast that you know you won't be able to play the difficult part. A mistake will not necessarily disappear when you know its cause; but you can improve much more quickly when you know what is wrong and are working effectively to correct it.

Beginners must always practise very carefully; it is often very difficult for them to play correctly, since they have so many things to consider and to remember, and may not know what a correct version is. So they must (as in fact all players must) concentrate very hard on the sound, constantly attempting to analyse what went wrong and why, and also attempting to improve their knowledge of good playing.

You will find it very helpful to listen to good performances. Broadcasts of recorder music are rare, but it is always easy to obtain gramophone records (and sometimes tapes and cassettes). Listen to them with care and attention, but don't allow yourself to be put off by the player's technique; he is, after all, a professional, and has spent many years learning to play so well. You have not had time to equal him—yet.

Once you know, for example, how a recorder should sound, you can begin to correct your tone. You can get some impression of how *you* sound by playing while facing a wall, provided you are not sitting too near; but it is far more useful to record your playing, if you have a recording machine which is good enough.

You can check your machine's reproduction of intonation by recording the standard tone that is broadcast on some radio or television stations before or after the programmes begin. A telephone call to your local station will tell you when the note is broadcast and whether it is standard A (440 cycles per second). If you record the first part of the tone and play back against the remainder, you can find out how accurately your machine reproduces and you will know what you are able to check with it. You can always use it to refer to rhythm, time, and aspects of interpretation. When it comes to performance, your most valuable assets are a good ear and a fund of experience. Your ear can be developed (see Chapter 17) and your experience will be increasing all the time.

Listening

An essential part of your practice is to listen to music attentively, trying to hear and to understand what is really going on. You will probably have a barrier to cross first: we are conditioned to think of music as something that goes on while we are doing something else. Concentrated listening is a strain, but if you try to listen with full attention to some music every day, it will become easier.

For beginners, particularly, criticism of their own playing is much easier if they are playing familiar music; but even at beginner level, correctness is only the first thing to attempt. Find, for instance, a record of a great singer performing a simple song. Listen to his performance, then try the same tune yourself. Concentrate on the differences between your performance and his or hers. You may not find this easy, but persevere; and do it more than once. There is always something more to be learnt from a good performance.

Learning theory

The amount of time during which you can really pay attention is limited, and it is much harder for a person teaching himself to keep his mind on the job than it is for a teacher to re-direct the attention of a pupil. Therefore, your practice should not be so long that you become bored; you should not be afraid to force yourself to continue work when you do not want to, but don't overdo it. Like most other skills, the power of learning improves with practice.

Also, remember that learning is not a continuous process; a graph of progress in learning goes up in steps; first a rise, then a level part; another rise, another levelling off; and so on. When you reach the level parts or 'plateaux', and no apparent progress is being made, you must continue to try. Suddenly, and often when you least expect it, you will start to progress again; and during the plateaux you are at least consolidating what you already know. This may be a reflection of your individual rate of learning and the fact that your mind is temporarily saturated. But if you are interested, your subconscious mind is still working at your problems, and they will be solved at some later date.

Mental attitude is very important. Natural musicians seem to be born with the correct attitude, and the periods of slog and hard work are easier for them than for the less-gifted. But hard work is inevitable at some stage, and the more you are mentally prepared for it, the easier it will be. Stay optimistic; things will come right in the end.

Standards

Your aim must always be perfection, even if it is perfection in the future. Whatever you play must be done as well as you know how, and you must always be alert to ways of improving your performance. Professionals have to be perfect every time; they are up against the standards of records and films, where each separate piece can be repeated until it is perfect, and all the perfect parts joined up to make one perfect whole. If you can't yet reach that standard, remember that amateur music sometimes has a freshness and vitality that is not always present in professional performances, and that a live performance, even with mistakes, can be better than a recording.

Exercises to help you

Exercises for breathing, tonguing, independence of fingers, and so on, can be found in the relevant chapters; but if you do have a specific problem, there is no reason why you should not make up your own exercises, particularly written musical ones. The standard exercise for learning a new note (Figs. 31 and 32) is only one of the things that can be done. But it is advisable first to know what you are attempting to do, and to construct the exercise in such a way as to make it as helpful as possible.

Practising a piece

When you are doing this, you can waste much time if you are not clear in your mind what you are trying to do.

First comes technical mastery, then interpretation of the composer's intentions, and last, at a later stage, your own interpretation.

Begin in the usual way, using speed as a check on what you find difficult, and playing in strict tempo against a metronome. Identify the difficult passages. It is sometimes useful to mark (in pencil) the passages to which you want to pay particular attention.

Once you are able to play the notes correctly, it is time to consider what the composer wants you to do. Make sure that you understand whatever directions he may have given you. Some of the commoner directions can be found listed in the Glossary; if the words you want are not there, consult one of the many musical dictionaries; *Rudiments of Music*, published by the Associated Board (see Further Reading) is a useful work.

The composer or editor will probably have given you some indication of the structure of the music by breath-marks. These must be followed.

The more you know about the structure of the music (see Chapters 14, 22, Further Reading) the better. The more you play and the more you listen to other performers, the more you will understand, and a basis of theory is very helpful.

Prepare your beginnings and endings carefully; if you are playing with anyone else, arrange for a signal at the beginning and end, and practise these until you are both, or all, doing exactly the same thing at the same time.

Be exact with your rhythms. A very common mistake, for instance, is to play a dotted quaver followed by a semiquaver as a quaver followed by a semiquaver. And be sure to give your rests their correct lengths.

Practice is preparation for performance. To my mind, music is not complete until the triangle of composer, performer, and audience is assembled; by constant repetition and concentrated thinking, prepare yourself to make the maximum effect on your audience.

SECTION 3

8 Technique (*Advanced*)

This chapter gives an overall view of the technique covered in this section. Individual aspects are dealt with in more detail in subsequent chapters.

Technique and speed are sometimes thought to be the same thing, but there is much more to it than that. If you have a good technique you should be able to play almost anything well, though not necessarily at sight.

The ear (*Chapter 17*)

It is essential to develop the ear, not only in technical matters such as intonation, but also in taste. This can best be done by acute, concentrated, critical listening to the best performers—and you need not restrict yourself to recorder-players. It will also help to read technical books on music and good music criticism, and to attend live concerts.

Fingering (*Chapters 3, 12 and 13*)

Some changes to and from notes are more difficult than others. When you meet difficulties, you must analyse and correct your faults. Sometimes poor changes are due to a lapse of memory or because a fingering is not well enough known to make the finger-movements instinctive; in other cases the fingers may not be sufficiently independent. All fingerings should be automatic, including alternative and trill fingerings.

If you have difficulty with a particular fingering or change, it is important to find out why. Exercises and repetition will eventually cure the trouble, but you will be able to deal with it much more quickly if you know the exact cause.

Tonguing *(Chapter 9)*

Natural ability to tongue varies; and it may require much work to develop good tonguing. To a great extent this is a matter of developing the control of the muscles involved and although all muscles can be trained and developed, some players will always have to work harder than others.

Breath *(Chapters 6 and 10)*

Subtle use of the breath is a mark of the advanced player. Phrasing, accent and expression all depend on the breath, as, to a large extent, does intonation. You should make every effort to develop your knowledge of music so that you know how you are using your breath, and why. The more often and the more critically you listen to good performances, the more your taste and knowledge will develop.

Speed

Increased speed is not only a matter of finger independence and control. Speed comes from: (a) the development of the muscles and reflexes; (b) the ability to synchronise the tongue and fingers; (c) experience, as you become more familiar with a wider range of patterns of notes. Most players can play faster slurred than detached.

To develop speed you need to practise slowly at first, the aim being to make all the required responses automatic. The slightest degree of hesitation can ruin a fast passage, so if you have some fast playing to do, repeat the passage many times slowly to a regular beat, analyse the difficulty, and practise whatever needs practising.

Speed and accuracy should go hand in hand; the more accurately a fast passage is played, the greater will be the effect. You should therefore practise fast passages until you can play them faster than you need to—this will give you leisure not only to make them effective, but also to consider their musical effect.

With some players, difficulty with fast playing may come from difficulty with fast reading. Experience is the greatest help here, but when you come across a passage which you had difficulty in reading, make sure that as soon as possible you study it until you do understand it.

Expression

Most music conveys emotion, and if you want to commun'cate emotion you must first feel it yourself, and then study how to convey your feelings to an audience. One way of doing this is to analyse effective performances; another is to try out various methods and see which is the most effective. I think it is important to cultivate the power of feeling the emotions that the music arouses in you, but the following are useful technical means of expressing emotion:

(1) Long notes can be varied in tone and volume. The recorder puts limits on what can be done, but you must use those limits.
(2) Volume and tone can be varied within a phrase. To some extent the recorder does this for you, as tone and intensity vary throughout its range; but, again, you must be able to use and to modify this.
(3) Time may also be varied within a phrase (see *Rubato*, Chapter 15).
(4) Do not neglect the possibilities of contrast. Where a phrase is repeated, never play it exactly the same way twice. Contrasts of volume can be extremely effective.

It is not possible to be precise about the emotional effect you will produce on your audience, since different people react differently to the same technique. Experiment as much as you can.

Style *(Chapter 20)*

This varies with period; a modern piece should not be played in the same style as a sixteenth-century galliard. The more you know about styles, the better you will play; and since much recorder music is dance-music, it will pay you to learn something about the dances of various periods. There are now many books on ancient dances and they can be obtained through libraries in all major countries.

9 Tonguing (*Advanced*)

When you have mastered single-tonguing and double-tonguing, it is time to consider other aspects of tonguing, particularly the artistic possibilities that exist in the infinite shades of expression that the tongue can make with the different consonants used.

Between 'T' and 'D' lie many different ways of shaping and ending a note. 'T' is in general crisp and light; 'D' is softer and heavier; and you can use as many shades of tonguing between them as can be distinguished. Also, 'D' can be made even softer; German books write this as 'DH'.

Experiment with all the shades of tonguing that you can manage, and listen very carefully for differences. As your ear develops you will be able to hear more. If you are trying to interpret the music, you will be using different tonguings in any case, however unconsciously; and as you learn more about music, so you will need more shades of expression.

You should experiment with the control of each of the four main consonants—T, D, K, and G; from the staccatissimo note which is sounded for as short a time as possible, to the tongued legato, in which the notes are barely (but distinctly) separated.

There is also combination tonguing (double and triple), in which you will want to find out which set of consonants you will prefer to use, and to develop your facility in using them.

Ending

Staccato playing will bring out the importance of ending a note well. All that is necessary is to return the tongue to its original position, with the tip against the palate. Some authorities try to establish this habit by giving single-tonguing as 'TUT' or 'DU–D' or 'DU–Ð' (a voiceless 'D' to end the note); but in fast detached passages and in combination tonguing this can cause difficulty— try to say 'TUT–TUT' fast, pronouncing each of the four 'T's. In combination tonguing it is unwise to repeat a consonant if you want speed.

Double-tonguing

The most usual consonants used for this are 'T–K–' or 'D–G–', but there are others. You can use 'TOOTLE', or, in certain cases 'T–R–' (see Specialist tonguings, below). Quantz (1752) used 'DID'LL'; Devienne and Hugo (1820) used 'TUTEL' and said that they had never heard 'D–G–' used successfully; but the two standard versions are best, unless there is special cause to use one of the others.

Triple-tonguing

For fast playing in three-time, the normal tonguings are 'T–K–D–', 'D–G–D', and 'T–K–T', but those combinations which require a repeated consonant are slower and more tiring than others.

The note on the beat should be slightly emphasised, and remember that in both double- and triple-tonguing the first consonant belongs to an accented note. Should your music begin on an unaccented note, you must use a secondary consonant (Fig. 37). Triple-tonguing only applies to groups of three notes (Fig. 38).

Fig. 37

Fig. 38

The artistic uses of tonguing

When you have mastered the basic tonguings and have learnt to apply them according to the rhythm or speed of the music, then it will be time to consider suiting your tonguing to the character, the mood, and the interpretation of the piece.

Your ear can tell you how your use of a given tonguing alters the artistic effect, and as your experience grows you will become better able to choose. What tonguings you use eventually must depend on your ideas of interpretation and your taste; these will be formed by what you listen to, by what you are taught, or by what you learn from other people you play with. In the main, listen to the best players you can find, and choose between them as wisely as you can; but do not imagine that what you have chosen today is necessarily fixed for all time.

Specialist tonguing

The conventions of French eighteenth-century music (and sometimes those of other places and times) are quite complex. Composers and players of the period understood that certain combinations of notes were not to be played exactly as written (quite apart from ornamentation). For instance, a descending passage of short notes (Fig. 39) would 'always' be played unevenly (Fig. 40), and tongued in the manner shown, the 'R' being emphasised and on the beat. Some composers and performers did not follow these conventions, and if you want to know more about them you will find a list of reference books on pages 160–161.

Fig. 39

Fig. 40

Some modern editions of music give what was intended by the composer rather than what was actually printed at the time, but beware of older editions which may not.

It is worth remembering that until recently much was left to the taste of the individual performer, and that this taste was governed by the prevailing style and the conditions of the performance, so that two performances of the same work might differ both from each other and from the original. Of course, taste was different at different periods. For example, this tune was published in the mid-eighteenth-century:

Fig. 41

The public taste of that time and place disapproved of movement by leap, so nearly all the leaps were filled in by ornaments to give an almost completely step-wise progression.

Fig. 42

When you have sufficient facility and experience, try playing a piece with as many different styles of tonguing as you can.

Slurring and tonguing

Slurring and tonguing help to avoid monotony in music and to make the grammar of the music clearer. The ways in which they are used are therefore very important. In the following extract (Fig. 43) (eighteenth-century), the composer marked in these slurs:

Fig. 43

If you play this as written and then experiment with other slurrings and tonguings, you will discover for yourself how much the character of the piece can be varied.

Almost any book on wind technique spends much time on slurring and tonguing, and usually gives many combinations. These should all be practised, but what they convey can be reduced to a fairly simple set of rules:

(1) Slur and tongue with respect for the beat and the phrase.
(2) Use your strongest tonguing on the notes you want to emphasise.
(3) The particular combinations of slurring and tonguing you use should depend on:
    (*a*) The composer's intentions;
    (*b*) The character of the music;
    (*c*) Your own taste.

When you have experimented with slurring and tonguing, look at as many pieces as possible and try to understand why the composer used the particular combinations he did. If you can obtain an *Urtext* of Bach's unaccompanied 'Cello Suites' (i.e. what Bach actually wrote), compare it with edited versions and with recorded performances. The differences can be remarkable.

Flutter-tonguing

This effect is used occasionally, for example in Benjamin Britten's 'Noye's Fludde'. Begin your note with an aspiration, almost an 'H'-sound, and vibrate your tongue as if you were rolling an 'R'. When you have this under control, try to get rid of the initial aspiration; then try to fit notes to the flutter.

10   The Use of the Breath *(Advanced)*

An advanced player needs to control his breath more strictly, and to use it in a more musical fashion, than can be expected from a beginner.

Breathing

The first step in learning breath-control is to find out your limits, and then extend them.

The amount of breath that you can take in is limited, not by the capacity of your lungs, but by the volume that you can handle. If you pump your lungs full of air, you may not be able to reduce your first exhalation to the amount required by the recorder.

It is also wise to practise emptying your lungs before filling them. If you have a succession of long phrases, and fail to empty your lungs properly before breathing in, you can collect carbon dioxide in the base of your lungs, and this can lead to fainting.

Make it a part of your practice to take deep breaths and let them out gently through the recorder, and also practise playing longer and longer phrases in one breath. In these ways you will begin to learn breath-control. You can also practise deep-breathing, letting the air out slowly and gently. Yoga and singing classes can help.

Secondly, try to strengthen your diaphragm. A useful basic exercise is to pant sharply and heavily, grunting as you do so. When you have got used to this, reduce the vocal noise. Any good singing tutor will give you more such exercises.

Thirdly, make sure that you are not leaking air through your nose or past your recorder because your lips have not sealed round it.

You should also try to increase the steadiness of your breath-pressure: you must be able to play long notes with steady intonation. As you exercise your diaphragm, this will become easier.

Your tongue is part of the apparatus of breath-control and you will find it helpful to practise tonguing with your breathing exercises.

All breathing in or out must be done quickly. Do not breathe through your nose; open your mouth and take breath quickly.

Very long phrases do occur. I give one here, which the music really demands you should play in one breath, though it is possible to take a breath (and miss out one semiquaver) at the place marked A.

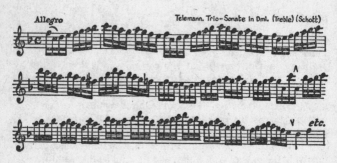

Fig. 44

Musical applications

You must understand the structure of a piece of music before you can really use your breath musically: breath taken in the wrong place could make nonsense of it. Most composers and editors insert breath-marks, and it is usually wise to follow them (see Sections 5 and 6 for more material on the structure of music).

Always try to understand why breath-marks are placed where they are and note the difference that the placing of a breath-mark or slur can make; you will learn much about musical structure in the process.

Fig. 45

Use your ear as a guide. You have probably heard a great deal of music in your life, most of it in the Western tradition. You are conditioned to expect certain patterns and to regard them as 'correct'. But this conditioning may not have been of a high enough standard of taste to enable you to judge what is good and what is bad. Listen to the best music and the best performers as much as you can; as your knowledge and experience increase, particularly if you listen intently and try to understand, your own critical standards will improve.

In your own playing, always think ahead; you should know what is coming next, and be preparing for it. Above all things, take breath before you intend to use it, and in the quantity that you require.

11 Practice *(Advanced)*

I believe that good technique is the first essential in playing any
instrument. If you can't play a passage adequately, or if you
suspect that you can't quite manage it at the speed at which it
should be taken, then you will not be able to do the music justice;
only when the technique is secure can you concentrate on the
musical qualities. Moreover, the knowledge that a doubtful
passage is coming can, and frequently does, produce tension;
and tension is the enemy of good playing. Consequently I have
given technique fuller consideration in Chapter 8 and have concentrated here on other aspects of practice, particularly those
relating to playing in consort or with an accompanist.

The main purpose of practice or rehearsal is to settle all the
details of performance between all the players concerned. Experienced players can, it is true, adjust to improvisation or unexpected changes, and even to mistakes; but it is much better to
do without them, even though a degree of improvisation can add
to the effect of a performance.

Memorisation

A professional player will prefer to memorise his programme,
since to memorise a piece gives one an incomparable freedom to
interpret. Even if you do not have opportunities to perform, you
should make a serious attempt to memorise one or two pieces, if
only for the experience.

Most of us already have some melodies memorised, and can
sing, whistle or hum them; but if you try to play them on your
recorder it may not come so easily. I suspect that this is because
most of us have to think of 'recorder technique'—of what notes
to play—whereas when singing, whistling, or humming, we are
not conscious of the means by which we produce the sounds.

How you start to memorise depends on your abilities and

knowledge. Some people use sheer repetition; others sit down and analyse the piece; others take it a little at a time. To some lucky ones it seems to come naturally.

One of the most recommended systems of memorisation is to try first to learn the piece as a whole, not bit by bit. When you have its overall design established in your mind, learn the parts that have proved more difficult to memorise one by one, but frequently play the whole piece, so that the design remains fresh in your mind.

Interpretation

Start by playing your piece several times, beginning slowly as usual, and looking for mistakes. Then analyse the mistakes and set them right. You should, in the end, be able to play your piece perfectly, faster than you are going to perform it.

When you are quite at ease with your piece, start to decide how you are going to play it. Follow the composer's marks to begin with; if you later decide that you are going to do it differently, make sure that you have good reason for what you do. Then mark your copy, and practise it according to your markings. Make these in soft pencil, BB at least, in case you change your mind; and make the markings bold, so that you can see them easily. Also, use an eraser to remove old markings, and avoid overloading the score with pencil marks.

When you are satisfied with your version, try it over with your accompanist. Make sure that he understands your markings, and transfer them to his score. Discuss them with him, and see whether any should be changed to fit his instrument or style.

Try to show the overall design of the piece. Find out where the climax is, and make sure that you play it as a climax. Take particular care over beginnings and endings.

See also Section 5, which will help you with some particular questions of interpretation.

Achieving balance with an accompanist

This is one of the most difficult things to achieve with the recorder. The instrument's tone has a penetrating quality through most of its range, particularly with the smaller recorders, but the lowest notes can quite easily be drowned. Your accompanist will have to be very alert to obtain a true balance at all times and still do justice to the music.

Do not attempt to assess balance by recording; too much depends on the position of the microphone. If you ask anyone to listen and to advise you, make sure that they are musicians and that they understand the problem. In the end you will have to use your own judgement as to what is a reasonable balance, and this will improve with experience.

If you are performing, remember that the acoustic qualities of a room can change dramatically when the audience is seated. As a general rule, a resonant room requires more detached playing.

Dynamics

Contrary to popular belief, the recorder can achieve changes of dynamics. For most practical purposes, the recorder can vary between *mf* and *mp* without noticeable change of pitch, even though the higher part of its range can be regarded as *f* or even *ff*. Greater changes can be managed by the use of alternative fingerings; for instance a very quiet F (descant), B flat (treble), can be managed by using fingering 01234 and very little breath; but this requires much practice and skill. It is also possible to have a key fitted to allow pianissimo playing.

It should be remembered that, even where the recorder part is marked 'Solo', the recorder should not always be the dominating instrument in a duet, and that in consort playing the most important part of the music is not always written for the highest instrument. Be prepared to give way where necessary.

Phrasing

You and your accompanist should agree on phrasing and take particular care over similar phrases. If, for instance, your accompanist has a phrase which echoes or imitates one of yours, they should normally be played (and ornamented) similarly. See also Chapter 14.

Ornaments

Even a beginner or intermediate player should be using the mordents and the trill, and an advanced player should have more in his repertoire (see Chapter 16). Whatever ornaments you are going to use should be agreed upon with the other player or players, and marked in all parts, until you reach the fairly advanced stage where you can improvise ornamentation and your partners follow suit.

The degree and type of ornamentation to be used is always a matter for argument, and really depends on the period, the composer, and your taste. Ornamentation can be overdone, but it can also be underdone, and, in my opinion, many modern performances are under-ornamented. The Further Reading section lists some specialist books in this area.

SECTION 4

12   Fingering Charts

The tablature used here is self-explanatory. I have collected as many alternative fingerings as seem reasonable, and for each note have put the standard fingering first, i.e. at the left, where I have given more than one fingering.

Notice particularly that different fingerings may require different breath-pressures and you should experiment with breath pressure until the note is right.

In the trill fingerings, the crosses mark the finger or fingers that should be moved.

If, as is quite possible, one or more of the alternative fingerings does not suit you or your recorder, either use another, or experiment until you can find a suitable one. I have left some room for you to note down extra fingerings.

ALTERNATIVE FINGERINGS 1

ALTERNATIVE FINGERINGS 2

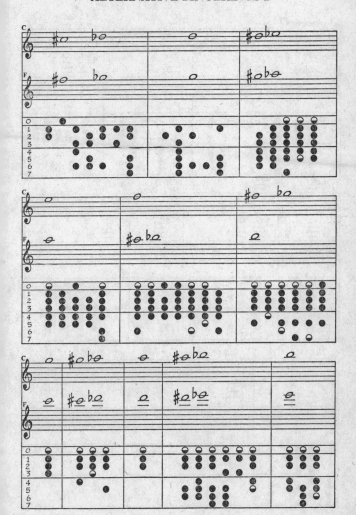

ALTERNATIVE FINGERINGS 3

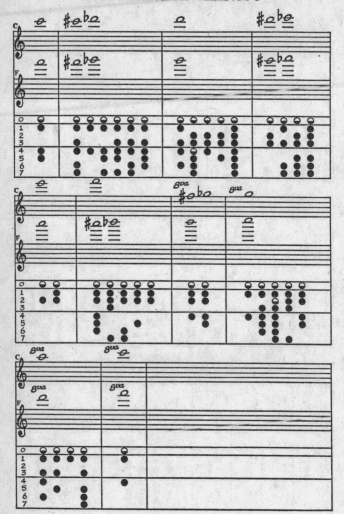

TRILL FINGERINGS 1

TRILL FINGERINGS 2

13   Technical Exercises

The exercises which follow are intended to help you to deal with various problems which are common to most recorder players. They are presented in the order in which I expect the difficulties to appear, so that you can use some of them almost from the beginning. The Descant exercises should be used by C recorder players, the Treble exercises by F recorder players (although space does not allow a separate section for basses).

Three types of exercises are given. The initial exercises are designed to help you learn new notes, and difficult changes between notes. The second set of exercises concerns tonguing and combinations of slurring and tonguing. Finally, there are exercises to practise velocity. These exercises can and should be played in all keys.

If you find that you can do an exercise well, leave it and pass on to another, coming back when and if you need it again. If you are learning a new note, use the exercise that belongs to that note in addition to any other material that you have in your tutor.

The exercises should be played as fast as possible *without mistakes*; if you are making mistakes, slow down. Aim to be able to play them all fast and fluently.

Play all the exercises with different combinations of slurring and tonguing, and also with changes of dynamics, making sure that the intonation does not change.

Alternative fingerings may be used with this material (see Chapter 12), and they may make some of the exercises easier; but practise them first with standard fingerings; alternative fingerings do not always produce the best notes. However, from the earliest stages, you should learn and use these two alternative fingerings:

Descant B, Treble E: 023

Fig. 46

Descant D¹, Treble G¹: 234567 or 1234567

Fig. 47

You should also practise these exercises with staccato and legato playing. To improve your staccato playing, take any exercise and progressively shorten the notes and increase the rest between each pair. Learn to produce the shortened notes cleanly and evenly, and make sure that your tongue and fingers synchronise. For legato playing, tongue more and more softly until the notes can hardly be heard to be separate; and practise all the degrees of staccato and legato that you can hear.

Double- and triple-tonguing may also be used, as appropriate.

As you become aware of what is lacking in your technique, there is no reason why you should not write your own special exercises, if your particular problem is not covered here.

DESCANT EXERCISES

DESCANT EXERCISES

DESCANT EXERCISES

TREBLE EXERCISES

TREBLE EXERCISES

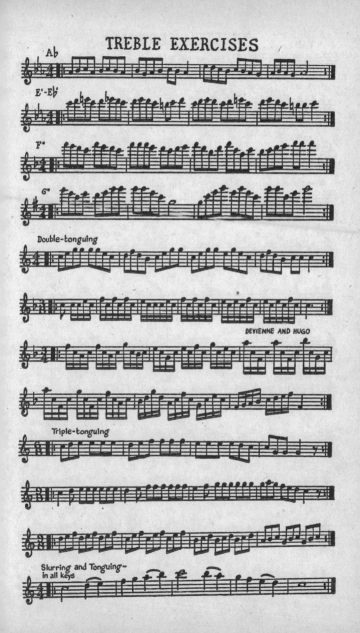

TREBLE EXERCISES

SECTION 5

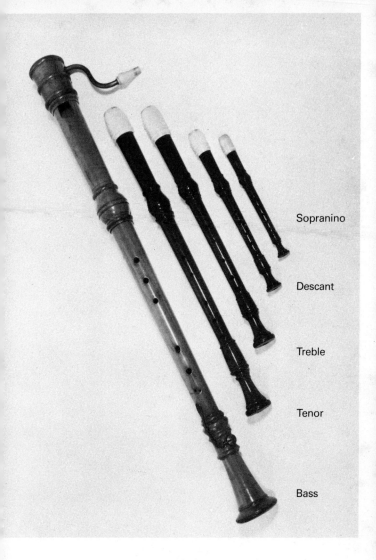

Sopranino

Descant

Treble

Tenor

Bass

PLATE 1
The Recorder Family

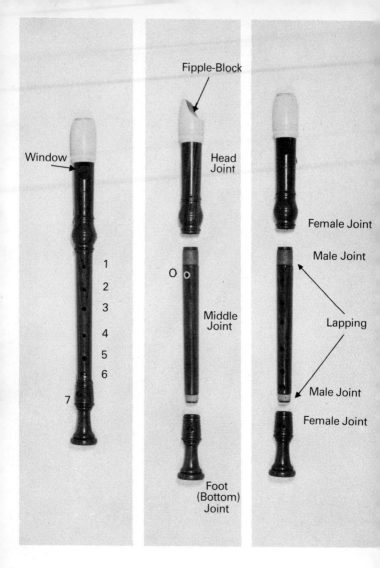

PLATE 2
The Parts of a Recorder (1)

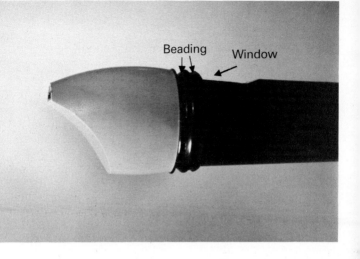

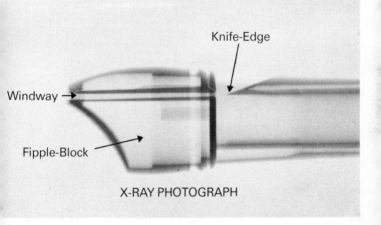

X-RAY PHOTOGRAPH

PLATES 3 AND 4
The Parts of a Recorder (2)

PLATE 5
The Hands – Playing Position

14 Phrasing

A book is punctuated into phrases, sentences and paragraphs which give meaning to the words. Music is organised in a similar way, but music needs more repetition than literature to convey its meaning. The phrase is one of the basic components of musical punctuation.

Singers' phrasing

Considering singing will help to make the meaning of phrasing clear. A singer, like a recorder-player, can only produce a limited number of sounds without taking breath; and he takes a finite time to breathe, which makes a break in the melodic line.

Since singers normally use words, this breathing is related to the sentence-structure and the sense of the lyrics, and sometimes to the emotion the singer wants to invoke. In the music shown in Fig. 48, the singer will breathe at the end of the second line, at

Fig. 48

least, and may breathe at the end of each line, since the punctuation requires him to make the slightest break there. In Fig. 49 the natural places for breath are fairly obviously indicated by the sense and punctuation. But the verse may be taken in two-line groups, whereas the chorus should be phrased in single lines, and within these lines there are many opportunities to increase the effect by slight breaks and stresses, and in many other ways. Think how you would sing it yourself.

Fig. 49

Instrumental phrasing

Where we are dealing with music without words, the guides to breathing are less obvious. In Fig. 50 the general structure of the phrases is indicated by the rests, but in bars 6, 10, 11, and 12 the composer or editor has decided that a breath-mark is necessary, even though it is not absolutely essential to take a breath at these points.

The above markings have probably been based on the general rules of of phrasing, which are as follows:

Most phrases are natural units; they 'sound right'; and as you play more and more music, you will become accustomed to recognising them. The ends of phrases are often marked by a

Fig. 50

rest, a long note, or a breath-mark (in music for wind instruments).

Music is frequently written in phrases of more or less equal lengths, which balance one another (Fig. 51).

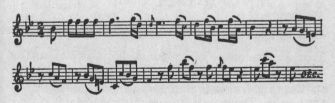

Fig. 51

Phrases may be short or long, but the tendency is for them to be in whole-bar units. Where they overlap a bar-line, their relative positions in the bar-structure tend to balance out.

A phrase is a complete musical idea which may be developed —indeed, it must be, or the piece will become dull. See how the original idea develops in Fig. 52.

Mozart. "Turkish Rondo"

Fig. 52

Pointing phrases

When you can identify phrases, you must begin to make use of them. If you were reading aloud, you would use inflection, changes of speed, volume, and emphasis in order to keep your listeners' attention and you should follow the same principle when playing the recorder.

As you begin to recognise the phrases in your music, try out the possibilities and see which are the most effective, trying to get the most possible out of each phrase, but remembering that they are only a part of a whole structure.

Phrasing rules

There are a few general rules which can help your phrasing (but remember that there are always exceptions).

(1) When a phrase rises in pitch, it is usual to increase volume.
(2) A descending passage is often played diminuendo.
(3) Contrasting passages need contrasting playing.
(4) A long note should be varied in volume and/or tone.
(5) When a phrase is repeated, or when the next phrase resembles the first, it is wise to make a difference in them, often in volume.
(6) Last notes need pointing (emphasising).

(7) Phrases are distinct units, but they are only part of a whole. Do not separate them too much, and let the overall design show.

(8) When you repeat a whole section of music, do not make an exact repetition. Leopold Mozart said that a Da Capo should always be played faster the second time 'or else the audience will go to sleep'.

(9) At a double bar it is permissible to make the slightest delay in beginning the new section; this should be just enough to let the audience know that something is happening.

(10) Almost every piece of music has a climax, which is usually, but not always, at or near the end. Keep back a little intensity so that the climax shows itself.

(11) A rest is not merely a silence; it is part of the structure of the music, and can be a most telling part of a phrase. Give rests their full value.

(12) Within the phrase, consider where an accent should be placed. Unexpected stresses can be very telling.

(13) Often in keyboard music, and sometimes in recorder music, phrasing is indicated by long slurs. This does not necessarily mean that recorder-players should use the slur as they normally understand it.

(14) Phrasing can be a matter of personal interpretation only to a limited extent.

Finally, remember that a knowledge of harmony will increase your understanding of the structure of a piece and its interpretation.

15 Rhythm

Rhythm and metre are not the same thing. The regular pulsation of accented notes which is a feature of most Western music, and which is implied by the time-signature and bar-lines, is the metre; but within this framework there are other accents, or groupings of notes, which give the music life. Without rhythm, music can be very dull.

Stresses

Bar-lines and time-signatures indicate regular stresses. There is always a stress on the first beat of the bar, and in other places according to the time-signature and the style, or according to special instructions. In $\frac{4}{4}$, the accent is strongly on the first beat and less strongly on the third; in $\frac{3}{4}$, strongly on the first; in $\frac{6}{8}$, strongly on the first and fourth quavers.

Most of these patterns of stresses are almost instinctive with us; we respond to them naturally, and music which is not stressed in this way does not seem right. In jazz and other related types of music, the accent seems to come on the 'off-beats'—the second and fourth beats—though I would suggest that at least some of this effect is due to the shortening of these beats; it is this feature, probably descended from country-dance playing, which helps to give life to the music.

But where the time-signature is 'unusual' as in $\frac{5}{8}$, the composer frequently has to indicate, either by stress-marks or by the way in which he writes the notes, the particular pattern of stresses he requires. $\frac{5}{8}$ can be stressed in several ways (Fig. 53), which turn it into a combination of $\frac{2}{8}$ and $\frac{3}{8}$, though there are true five-in-a-bar rhythms, as in Tchaikovsky's Sixth Symphony (the Valse movement), Brubeck's 'Take Five', or in some English folk-songs.

Fig. 53

Stresses implied by the music do not have to be shown; but exceptions are indicated in a variety of ways, among which are the various stress-marks (page 134).

There are some cases where music changes its time-signature so frequently that a composite time-signature is the only possible answer (Fig. 54), and some national music has time-signatures that are still strange in the Western world (Fig. 55). Notice how the stresses are indicated by the grouping of the notes.

Fig. 54

Fig. 55

Grouping notes

Patterns of stresses can be indicated by the grouping of written notes within the bar; normally there will be a slight stress on the beginning of each group.

Fig. 56

Fig. 57

Fig. 58

Fig. 59

Note groupings are often helpful indicators of how the music should be played. In Fig. 60 you know that the first group of notes has to be played in the time of one minim, and that the first note is stressed.

Fig. 60

Rhythm in performance

The subtle pointing of a phrase by accent, or in many other ways, is best learnt by listening to good players. When a first-class wind-player comes to your area, get an advance copy of the programme, obtain a copy of one of the pieces to be played, and study it; if possible, practise it until you are playing it as well as you can. Then take the music with you to the concert, and listen to the shaping of the phrases, the variations in speed and volume, to all the subtle differences between the work of a great artist and that of an ordinary player. Try to work out where the difference lies. Alternatively, do the same with a gramophone record.

Do not attempt to reproduce anybody else's particular interpretation, except for study purposes; to do this would be to turn yourself into a machine. The ability to make your own interpretation will come with experience.

Rubato

Rubato means, literally, 'stolen time'. A barrel-organ or a musical-box produces a cheerful, accurate performance, but it lacks humanity, because it is too exact. In a live performance, the performer slightly alters the length of some of the notes for the sake of expression. Notes are lengthened, stressed, or shortened as the desired effect requires, with important notes emphasised more than is shown in the printed score.

The time 'stolen' by rubato must be paid back, as otherwise the metre of the music will be distorted. Mozart insisted that rubato in the melody must take place over an unvarying bass, and true rubato takes place in short phrases only, and preferably within the bar.

The amount of alteration permissible has varied at different times. In the seventeenth century, for instance, time in singing was subject to the sense of the words:

> 'Then we take Liberty (and very often, for Humour and good Adornment's sake, in certain Places) to Break Time; sometimes Faster and sometimes Slower, as we perceive the Nature of the Thing requires, which often adds much Grace and Luster to the Performance.'
>
> (*T. Mace*, 1676)

Couperin, in the same century, said that the time of set pieces should not be altered, nor notes held for longer than their true values; J. J. Quantz, heir to an older tradition, wrote in 1752 about the extent to which written music did *not* represent what would actually be played. Amongst other things, he wrote that a string of shorter notes should be played unequally, dwelling on the notes which came on the beat and shortening slightly those that came off the beat.

Unless you are exceptional, you probably use rubato, perhaps unconsciously, because it seems to be an instinctive way of expressing feeling. What matters is whether it is well or badly done, and here again listening to professionals will help you.

Lift

Listen, if you can, to a good folk-dance player. He gives the dancers a 'lift' by subtly accenting the tune. An exact reproduction of the written notes would have nowhere near the same effect. There are of course many clichés in folk-dance playing which are not suitable for other types of music—the glissando, the strong accent on the beat and the slight clipping of unaccented notes; but if you listen to a bad player also, you will soon begin to appreciate where, and why, the better player is different. Neither loudness, speed, nor technique makes the difference between good and bad players; the difference lies in the stressing of important notes, the lightening of unimportant ones, and the almost imperceptible lengthenings and shortenings that are used. A good player is feeling the dance and expressing it in his music.

Many recorder-players play dance-music of the sixteenth to eighteenth centuries. I am firmly of the opinion that early dance-music should have 'lift', but far too often, in modern performances, the playing is too constrained and exact.

Syncopation

In syncopation, the rhythm lies across the beat. If you find a syncopated rhythm difficult, count *one-and-two-and*, stressing whichever '*ands*' are required. It is better to feel and enjoy the syncopation, but most of us have to come through the '*one-and-*' stage.

Where the rhythms really clash (for example, in galliards, where $\frac{6}{4}$ or $\frac{6}{8}$ frequently clash with $\frac{3}{2}$ or $\frac{3}{4}$) it is easy to get confused, particularly when you are relying on counting to keep your place, but you will in time progress to the point where you are able to feel the clash and enjoy it.

Dowland (Schott)

Fig. 61

16 Ornaments

The information given in this section is necessarily limited. If you want to study ornaments fully, consult some of the books suggested on the Further Reading list. The question of ornamentation is problematical for four reasons. Firstly, ornaments varied in their names, styles, content and written symbol at different periods. Secondly, some composers used different ornaments and written symbols at different times in their lives. Thirdly, some composers wrote their ornaments out in full, some only used a symbol meaning 'ornament required here', and some did not mark in the ornament at all. Fourthly, the choice of whether or not to ornament, and of which ornament to use, has generally rested with the performer. His choice was governed by the prevailing standards of good taste, and that good taste varied in different countries and at different times.

General rules

In spite of the confusion, there are some general rules about ornamentation, and some ornaments, that can usefully be given here.

Ornaments are used to point a particular note, to give freshness and spontaneity to a performance, occasionally to herald a change in harmony, to improve the ends of phrases, and generally to improve what might otherwise be a plain melody.

If you follow the recorded performances of great players with the score, study what music with written ornaments comes your way, and use your commonsense, you should be able to produce a well-ornamented performance.

Ornamentation can be overdone, but players today are more likely to under-ornament than to use too many. Consider this melody and its ornamented version.

Fig. 62

The following list includes the ornaments you are most likely to meet. There is sometimes great confusion over names. For instance, the mordent and inverted mordent which follow are correctly named for the eighteenth century; but if you are taking musical examinations today the names are reversed. What matters, however, is that you should use them well and with a sense of correct style.

Mordents

One of the most useful ornaments is the mordent. Its most usual form is a little flick of the note under the written note (Fig. 63).

Fig. 63

It is used to point notes of importance, usually on the beat, and must be within the scale being used at the time; occasionally, for harmonic reasons, it may be out of the scale, in which case the composer often indicates his intentions as in Fig. 64. This ornament, like most others, should start on the beat, not before it.

Fig. 64

Inverted mordent

This is the reverse of the mordent, but is usually played with a double flick; it starts on the note above the written note (Fig. 65).

Fig. 65

Appoggiatura

The 'long appoggiatura' is a most effective ornament, and may come from above or below the written note (Fig. 66). Its powers of expression come from the clashes of harmony it may produce, and from the fact that it delays the cadence, since it may take as much as two-thirds of the length of the written note before it resolves. It is often used with last notes, and must begin on the beat.

Fig. 66

The 'short appoggiatura' may be used to fill in leaps, and is normally accented.

Fig. 67

Acciaccatura

This is a very short note, flicked in from above or below, and it should be played on the beat.

Fig. 68

Trill

Every wind-player should be able to trill well. Styles of trilling vary with the periods, but in general a trill should be a rapid alteration of the written note with another, usually the one above it in the scale or, more rarely, below it, and very occasionally a major or minor third away.

Fig. 69

Trills may be short, in which case they resemble the inverted mordent, or long; as a general rule in Elizabethan and eighteenth-century music, start on the note above the written note.

Trills must be clear and regular, though in some cases it is very effective to start slowly and accelerate. The movement is usually within the scale; where it is not, an accidental is written with the trill sign (which is most commonly *tr*) over or under the sign.

For recorder-players, some trills are very difficult to play with standard fingering, and you should consult the special table of trill fingerings in Chapter 12 if you have problems.

Trill and turn

Sometimes, in order to finish a trill better, it is ended with a turn.

Fig. 70

Scale passages

At times large leaps were not regarded with complete favour, and could be filled in with a running passage, as in Fig. 71. Such passages would normally be within the scale.

Fig. 71

Broken chords

A long last note or a final cadence would often be filled in with a flourish, which sometimes resembled a cadenza. For your own purposes, you can use a broken chord occasionally to point the last note, as in Fig. 72, but do not overdo it.

Fig. 72

As you learn and begin to use ornaments, they will become easier and more natural, and eventually you may arrive at the stage where ornamentation is so natural that you may find it difficult to play the written notes only. This is good—ornamentation should be used—but you must stay within the bounds of good taste. It is helpful, in deciding where these bounds lie, to study composers such as Couperin, who wrote their ornaments out in full or who used a vocabulary of special signs, and to look at modern editions which do the same. You may find experts who will disagree with any ornamented version, for ornamentation is and was always a question of personal choice.

17 Aural Training

Some people are born with the ability to identify a musical sound instantly; they are able to tell you the letter-name of any note that they hear, and can sing, at the correct pitch, any music that they read. This is not an unmixed blessing, but those who have this ability do have an advantage in many forms of music-making. Others have an extraordinary musical memory. Most of us are not so lucky; we have abilities, and they can be developed, but we will not be able to reach those standards.

Basic abilities

Making music does demand some basic abilities. If you are unable to hear differences of pitch, then you are never likely to play in tune.

But you must beware of assuming that, because you have difficulties now, you will always have them. Some difficulties, it is true, cannot be overcome because the equipment required is not there, but the great majority of people can improve their abilities, depending on the amount of work they are prepared to put into it.

Instrumental training demands the ability to hear the finer distinctions of pitch and of rhythm, and to have a well-developed musical memory. These can all be improved and there are some guidelines which can help you.

Improving intonation

Whenever you listen to music, listen with as much concentration, and as critically, as you can. This is difficult to keep up at first, but the more you do the easier it will become. Start with short periods of concentrated listening, and work up to longer ones. Listen to tapes or records if you can, because you can play them again. First, listen to the melody, because it is usually the easiest thing to follow, and then try to hear the other parts. Choose an instrument that has a distinctive tone (for example, an oboe), and try to follow it through the piece (remembering that it may not be playing all the time). Then choose another, and follow that. Eventually you should be able to follow all or any of the parts through a performance.

Cultivate a sense of the relationship between the written symbol and its sound. Most professional musicians can read a line of printed music and hear it in their minds. Many people can hear written harmony in their mind, and some can hear a full score.

This takes time and experience, but you should be able to hear simple music that you know quite clearly; and you can develop this ability by copying out familiar music, singing music that you already know from a score, and by trying to write down tunes that you know. The more you do, the more you will learn. Sight-singing simple tunes is well worth while.

You will be helped in your sight-singing by a knowledge of intervals (see Chapter 22), and you can help yourself still further by collecting familiar tunes that illustrate particular intervals. Some of my stand-bys are shown in Fig. 73.

Fig. 73

Improving the intonation of single notes

Experiment with your instrument. You know that if you increase the breath-pressure the note will sharpen. Play various notes with differing amounts of breath-pressure and try to hear the differences. Listen to an orchestra tuning up; try to follow a particular player as he tunes; listen to live performances for out-of-tune notes.

Teaching yourself to listen is the crux of the matter; through this you will develop your sense of intonation as far as possible within your limits.

Obtain (not necessarily buy) two A tuning forks, one at standard A (440 *c.p.s.*) and one at New Philharmonic pitch A (439 *c.p.s.*). Sound them one after another and see if you can hear the difference; then sound them together and hear the sounds fighting one another. Try again after a few months' practice in concentrated listening.

If you pull the top joint of your recorder out slightly, you will flatten its pitch. Try to hear the variations in the pitch of the note with the head in various positions. If you are playing with friends, experiment with common chords (see Chapter 22) with all except one player trying to maintain a steady note, and the individual varying his intonation.

Patience, perseverence, and concentrated listening will improve your sense of pitch. There is a limit beyond which you cannot go, but it is almost certainly higher than you think.

Improving rhythm

As a first step in improving rhythm, you must work at your sense of metre. Most music has a regular pulse, and most of these pulses come in twos or threes (four is a variant of two). Again, listen to music; but this time try to establish what its metre is. With some types of music this is easy; with others, hard—and the pulse may change. Use something simple to begin with. When you think you are right, try beating time, and see if your down-beat comes on the heaviest accents, which are usually at the beginning of a bar. A conductor's down-beat always comes at the beginning of a bar. Watch the conductor at concerts if you can, but do not be discouraged if his beating does not make a regular pattern.

Then find a regular pulse and fit to it music that you know—for instance, try to fit a familiar tune to the ticking of a clock, or to your footsteps as you walk.

When you can do this easily, as you probably can already, set yourself a harder task. Put on a record or a tape, establish the metre in your mind, and then turn the volume down to inaudibility. Turn it up again and see whether the pulse in your mind still fits that of the music. Or do the same with a metronome, which is easier to follow.

When you are playing, establish the habit of counting the beats in your mind. When you have rests, count carefully (but not aloud). You are trying to establish a subconscious habit of counting the beats in your mind, so that you always know where the best is, and so can stress it correctly.

When you have metre established, it is time to progress to rhythm. You must first, of course, get to know the written symbols of music; then you must start to collect rhythmic patterns, so that fewer and fewer take you by surprise. When you find something new, take time to work it out and learn it — there is no time for working out while you are playing. In the end you will have a vast stock of rhythmic patterns in your memory. Don't forget that music is written or printed to make this easy for you. To begin with, be as correct as possible; later on you can deal with the minute shades of rhythm that can make so much difference to a performance.

Developing memory

A musical memory is one of the most useful things that you can develop. For instance, you will not be able to compare the pitches of two successive notes unless you can remember both.

As a first step in developing memory, it is most important to listen and to hear clearly; if you hear a muddle, you will only remember a muddle. An important factor here is the extent to which you *want* to remember, and this is influenced by the amount of pleasure that you get from or associate with a tune. So start by memorising tunes that please you.

When you have heard music performed, sit back afterwards and think about it: How many instruments? What were they? Did they play all the time? What was the melody? What was the time-signature? If you can answer these questions, try to remember finer details. Then, if you are using a record, turn it on again and see whether you were right. Don't be afraid of becoming bored; if you have chosen the right music, there is always something more to discover.

18 Intonation

Pitch

I must start here with a statement which may seem somewhat puzzling at first: there is no note which has a fixed pitch except, in certain circumstances, standard A (in most countries, 440 cycles per second, *c.p.s.*); in playing, the pitch of any note may vary between bars and even between repetitions of the same note. The reasons for this are complex.

Try, when you can, this experiment. Use a recently-tuned (and correctly-tuned) piano. Play this sequence; tonic, leading note, tonic (see Chapter 22), shown in Fig. 74 in the key of C.

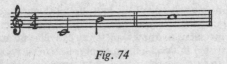

Fig. 74

Sing it with the piano several times. Then repeat it unaccompanied several times (you may sound the first note if you wish). Then, after your last unaccompanied version, sing it with the piano or listen to the piano notes. If your ear is reasonably good, you will almost certainly hear that the leading note (B, in this case), has sharpened as you sang it unaccompanied. This sharpening of the leading-note (see Chapters 21 and 22) occurs in all scales; and we also modify other notes according to their position in the scale, though the sharpened seventh is the most marked. Since many pieces of music modulate, or change key, a note which is the leading-note in one key will not be the leading-note in another key, and so must change its pitch.

Fifths are also altered. In order to establish a fifth firmly in your mind, listen to an orchestra tuning up (all the strings, except the double-basses, tune in fifths), or remember the first three notes of 'Baa, Baa, Black Sheep'.

Fig. 75

You may have to take my word for it, but eight correct fifths add up to more than five octaves, and, on a correctly-tuned piano, all the fifths are flat.

It is all concerned, of course, with the sound and effect that we expect from music. To our Western ears some harmonies sound better than others; when we play or sing we modify pitch in some places to produce sounds that are more pleasing to us.

Enharmonic tuning (being really in tune)

The first, and most necessary thing to remember is that leading-notes must be sharpened, and that the key of the music may change during a piece. The leading-note of the key in which the piece is written can be easily discovered (Chapter 22), but when there is a modulation—when the music moves into another scale—the new leading-note must be sharpened and the old one drops a little in pitch. Modulations are sometimes shown by a new key-signature, but more often by an accidental—a sharp, flat or natural added to the music. Adjustment for this is instinctive once you have recognised the new key, but a knowledge of harmony does help (Chapter 22), and it is true that if you play all scales with the intonation required for C major, the more remote scales will sound distressingly out of tune.

The tempered scale

This problem affected, and does affect, all keyboard-players. Instrumentalists can adjust for different keys; keyboard-players cannot, and a piano tuned for correct intonation in any key is only usable for a few closely-related keys. There is a system of tuning (the tempered scale) which allows a keyboard instrument to play in all keys without sounding out of tune, and J. S. Bach wrote his 48 Preludes and Fugues to demonstrate it. A piano is never really in tune in any key, although it sounds reasonably correct. It therefore cannot produce the sonorities and effects that can be produced by instruments which allow for enharmonic changes and are able to adjust the note according to its position in the scale.

Such advanced intonation is not always within the reach of beginners and intermediate players; they must use piano tuning until their ears and musical knowledge are sufficiently advanced.

Correcting faulty intonation

A solo beginner, playing unaccompanied, is unlikely to appreciate the delicate nuances of intonation, but as soon as he begins to play with others, the effects of incorrect intonation will soon be heard, particularly when there are three or four parts involved. In unison playing, particularly with a large group, incorrect intonation is less easily detected, but elementary quartets often develop what is called a 'resultant harmonic'—a tone unrelated to the music. Often this is caused by one player playing sharp, but it is always due to faulty intonation somewhere, and it is sometimes hard to correct. It disappears when each player becomes aware of his intonation and of that of the others, and each adjusts to fit the common pattern. The following exercises can help:

(a) Play in simple block harmonies—the simpler hymn tunes are useful—listening to all the parts. Watch particularly for players using the lower range; they are frequently sharp.
(b) Play scales or passages in unison. I have noticed that when you are playing in unison, and in tune, your own tone tends to disappear, and you hear the other player's.
(c) Where particular chords are not in tune, build them up from the bottom, listening carefully to the effect of each addition (Fig. 76).

Fig. 76

Some out-of-tune effects can be caused by excessive out-of-phase vibrato. Vibrato involves an alteration in pitch, in that the note played moves above and below the correct pitch. If only two players are involved, their pitches must move above and below at the same time, so that the relative distance between their notes remains the same. If they move above or below at different times, this distance can be exaggerated and sometimes produces distressing sounds.

Very occasionally, undesired harmonics are caused by using instruments of different makes or tunings. For example, while standard pitch is A = 440 *c.p.s.*, some tuners and makers use New Philharmonic (A = 439 *c.p.s.*) and I have met with instruments tuned to lower pitches.

Where it is necessary to correct intonation, it is usual to use breath-pressure; the higher the breath-pressure, the higher the pitch, and vice-versa. However, if used to excess, this method may affect tone, and so other methods sometimes have to be used.

Tuning

A recorder can be tuned to a certain extent. If you slide the head of the recorder out a little, you will lower the pitch of the whole instrument, though if overdone, this may affect different notes to different extents (remember also that you cannot *sharpen* the instrument in this way). Sometimes flatness is due to lack of warming-up. Before you play, warm the recorder by holding it in your hands, or tucking it under your armpit, or by blowing through it (taking care not to introduce excessive moisture).

Shading

If some notes on your recorder are out of tune, it is possible to gain better intonation by 'shading', which means covering or

part-covering other holes than those required for correct fingering (for instance descant E flat, treble A flat is normally fingered
234567, but some recorders require 1234567). If you finger
descant G, treble C, and gradually lower finger 4 on to its hole,
the note will gradually flatten; and if you raise finger 3, the note
sharpens. This principle can be applied to almost every note,
though it is not always the next finger that should be used. The
method should never be used without prior practice.

With the larger recorders, it is possible to use 'knee-shading',
where the bottom of the recorder is rested on the knee and the
hole at the bottom partially closed; but this is an unreliable
method unless you know exactly what you are doing. It is far
better to use the breath.

A surprising amount of correction to faulty intonation can be
obtained simply by thinking the correct sound, just as one tends
to play in a given manner by thinking the appropriate thoughts.

One thing is essential; to train the ear. It is the only guide to
correct playing (see Chapter 17).

If you are interested in the principles behind music, I can
thoroughly recommend *Sound Sense* by Geoffrey Russell-Smith,
for a readable elementary account of why music sounds the way
it does. Those who want to go further should read Alexander
Wood's *The Physics of Music*. Professor Seashore's *Psychology of
Music* also gives some surprising information about musical
abilities. See Further Reading.

19 Sight-Reading

Everybody has to sight-read (to play music at first sight) some time, but there is not necessarily any connection between the ability to sight-read well and musicianship, although, of course, the experienced musician is likely to be the better sight-reader.

This is mainly because he is much more familiar with the likely patterns of music. In your own home you do not have to consult an inventory to find out where your favourite chair is; you go to it. You can open your door and switch on a light much more quickly than a stranger can. You can deal with familiar processes more easily and quickly than a beginner can. The more music you read, the more easily you will sight-read.

If you want to be a good sight-reader there are a number of things that you can do. First of all, you need as much new music as possible. If you have learnt all your notes, you can play any music that keeps within the range of your instrument. So look around the house for any printed music that there is, borrow from libraries, or from friends. If you are buying music specifically for sight-reading, buy as cheaply as you can (and see Chapter 25).

The normal rules of practice do not apply to sight-reading; you must play to the beat, and leave out whatever you cannot manage at the time, or you will never be able to play at sight with other players. Of course, what you miss out when sight-reading should be studied later until you can manage it, but not *while* you are sight-reading. Use a metronome, when alone and make sure that the bell is correctly set—it is very easy to slip a beat when you are practising.

You must also become a better reader of music; you cannot afford to be baffled by something you have not seen before. Study the written language of music, and also try to widen your vision so that you are seeing more than the note, or group of notes, that you are playing. You are used to looking ahead when reading words on the page, and you should also do this when reading music. The smaller your field of vision, the more difficult it is to move your eyes over a large part of the page, and the more you will be taken by surprise by unfamiliar things. This is, of course, a matter of memory; you remember the notes that you are actually playing, while looking ahead to what is coming. The more music you have played, the more will be familiar to you.

Scales and arpeggios should be mastered, since they form the basis of many common patterns in music.

Preliminary work

When you are going to read at sight, you should take a little time to look the music over before you start to play. Time is always allowed for this in examinations, though it never seems enough. Memorise, of course, the key-signature, time-signature, and any other instructions the composer has seen fit to give you, and look as far through the piece as you can, looking for difficult passages, repeats and Da Capo's. It is customary to play the piece as written unless you have agreed otherwise. But don't waste time by looking over parts that you can play perfectly well.

Group sight-reading

If you are sight-reading with others, decide who is to lead—preferably your best musician or one who is playing from a score and knows how to read it. Preliminary beats are considered to be unprofessional.

Watch the other players as much as you can, particularly when two or more of you have to enter together—which implies that you must be able to memorise a group of notes. Also arrange for, and practise, clean endings.

Mistakes will occur, and sometimes one or more players will 'get lost'. As a general rule, you should not stop for them; their ability to re-find a lost place will develop with practice. But if there is hopeless confusion, stop and start again—more slowly. With experience you will be able to realise where you should be in your part, and adjust. This is sometimes particularly useful where you have a player who is convinced that he is right, and continues in his progress regardless of everybody else.

Entries

Be prepared for your entries. In some music, particularly poly-phonic music, you may not be required to start at the beginning, and you may find rests of several bars. If the publisher has not given you a 'cue' (i.e. notes of another part which signal your entry), it is often useful to pencil the other part in, since con-fusion is often caused where only one instrument enters and the other players do not know how long his notes are. It is often sufficient to show the note-lengths only.

Fig. 77

Keeping place

You must keep your place. This is easier when the parts are in a score, provided that you can read all the lines; but you must always be aware of the beat, which means that consciously or unconsciously you must both count and listen for metrical stresses. Avoid foot-tapping; if you must move something, move your toe inside your shoe.

Interpretation

As your powers of sight-reading improve, you should try to make your performance as good as you can, even on the first reading. You are unlikely to be able to sight-read perfectly, but you should make every effort to follow the composer's directions as you play.

Writing

Do not forget the value of copying out music in helping you to recognise and remember musical patterns. At first you will have to form the notes very carefully, but later on you will be able to write much faster, because you will have discovered what is essential to indicate a note. You must be particularly careful over the position of the heads of the notes; if the head is not exactly on a line or in a space, it can cause confusion. It is particularly valuable in the first stages to copy out music that you know as it teaches you to associate the symbol and the sound.

The limits of sight-reading

There are occasions where first-class sight-reading is essential: for an accompanist at the piano; for an operatic répétiteur; for a band which has to play request numbers; and sometimes for a pit orchestra; but some players attach far too much importance to sight-reading, and seem to want to have played everything in the recorder repertoire once. This will not help you to progress, as a satisfactory performance will only come with practice and thought.

Confidence

To some extent, sight-reading is a matter of confidence; a person whose confidence is easily shaken will have trouble sight-reading. But the confidence must be justified. The greater the knowledge of music, the easier sight-reading will become.

20 Style

'When I use a word,' Humpty Dumpty said, 'it means just what I choose it to mean.' The word 'style' is a case in point. It can cover, for example, individual qualities of performance, the way in which a piece is played, the way in which it should be performed, or the way of performing music of a given type.

Each musician has his own style; some performers, at least, can be recognised by the ear alone. Inevitably you will develop your own style, and you should make sure that it is a good one.

Style and interpretation are closely connected, and the first essential of style is to be able to do what the composer intended. Pay particular attention to his markings (though composers' metronome markings are sometimes inaccurate). When you can do what the composer intended, it will be time to consider whether you wish to alter this interpretation. Listen intently to your practice and beware particularly of unconscious alterations.

Period style

Quite apart from your individual style, you should be aware of the style or particular periods, so that you can approach the music of the time intelligently.

Early music
Definitions of 'early' vary, but here I refer to eleventh- to fifteenth-century music in general. Not much is known about the style of playing used by musicians of the period, and what is known is mainly deduced from the music and from pictures of players. There is little writing in harmony as we understand it today, and though there are some dances, much of the surviving music is Church music. If you play the Church music, you have good models in plainchant, and there are some recordings available. There are also recordings of secular music, though I think that

many of today's recordings of early music lack life and fun. They are very accurate and are often played on the correct instruments, but I am sure that the original performances had more rhythmic vitality and drive.

It seems likely that our ancestors had much more appreciation of tonal differences than we do; there are many families of instruments that have similar sounds, but were used and contrasted as groups in orchestras. Early music is also likely to have had a weakish bass line, owing to the fact that there were not many effective bass instruments.

If you know several players of early instruments, and you and they want to play together, it also seems quite legitimate to use several of the same kind of instrument—there could be several lutes in a band, for instance.

I would suggest that when playing early dance-music, you treat it as music intended for dancing, and try to give it a good lift and movement. Also, study the possibilities of adding percussion; it can give a new dimension in performance.

Renaissance music

Though some of the dance-music is four-square as in early music, this period mainly produced polyphonic music, which requires a different style. In general the parts are independent and equal in performance, and there is a considerable amount of imitation; one instrument plays a phrase which is imitated, usually at another pitch, by another. There is also much clashing, both of harmony and of rhythm.

There is also a tendency for middle parts to have a simple tune, and for other instruments to play a highly-complicated part above it, and sometimes below.

Try to balance up your parts so that each one can be heard equally well, and work towards the point where the players listen for imitations and follow the style set by the player of the first phrase, particularly in ornamentation. Enjoy the vigour of the music, don't be put off by the occasional harshness of the harmony, relish the clashes, and, if you are playing one of the decorated parts, be rhythmically accurate and neat in your playing.

Tudor music

In general, this is a development of Renaissance music. Some of the harmony is sweeter, but enjoy the clashes, and be particularly careful of your rhythm.

A good introduction to the style can be had by playing madrigals, of which many were written for voices and/or instruments. If you have a four-part consort available, play the voice parts. Alternatively, try a solo line and keyboard reduction. There are several publications available which give these reductions, and you might also be able to interest a lutenist or guitarist. There are lute accompaniments available to many madrigals.

In madrigals, it is the words that govern interpretation. Read them carefully and try to fit the music to the words. In the sixteenth and seventeenth centuries it was accepted practice to vary the speed and style of the music to suit changes in the meaning of the words.

You may also enjoy the visual effects in the music; for instance, any reference to 'down' or 'falling' might well be set to a downwards movement of the music.

The great thing to enjoy about 'Tudor' music (which did not die with Queen Elizabeth) is its enormous vitality, its tremendous interest in new discoveries, its love of ingenious devices, and its intricacy.

Late seventeenth-century music

Something happened to music in the seventeenth century, and a different style developed. Mace's 'Music's Monument' was published in 1676, and is old-style in the main. Henry Purcell was born in 1658/9, but the contrast between his music and Mace's is tremendous. The new music used a different, richer harmony, with much less clashing. When you play music of this type, give it all the tone you can, and be exceptionally careful over intonation.

'Eighteenth-century' music

I put this heading into inverted commas because it refers to a style rather than to dates. The music of Haydn, Mozart, and many others was in keeping with the ideas of their period: neatness, grace, beauty, and self-discipline. On the one hand, they wanted self-control, poise, and elegance; on the other, they sought to appeal to their listeners' emotions as powerfully as possible. When you play music of this period, don't think of it as pretty and shallow; the emotion is there, and much eighteenth-century music has the elegance of a gentleman's sword; it is beautiful, stripped down to essentials, and completely practical for its purpose. Give the music all the emotion you can, and remember that the dances of the period demanded elegance, poise, and beauty of movement, combined with a steely strength.

Victorian music

There is virtually no recorder music of the Victorian period, though you can find playable flute sonatas, and recorder music was still being produced in the Georgian period. The music of these times was often overly-sentimental for modern taste.

Modern music

There are too many styles in modern music for any general rules to be of much use. Pay particular attention to the composer's intentions as he expresses them; and be as accurate as you can. In general, unemotional treatment is often required.

Emotion

The most important element of a good style, that you can cultivate, is that of stirring the emotions. Music was always something that could be felt deeply; it was even thought that listening to music could affect the character. All the books by leading players and composers contain directions as to how the player can effect the emotions of his listeners.

'We had for our Grave Music, Fancies of 3, 4, 5, & 6 Parts . . . yet what can I best speak of Them, shall be only to say, That They have been to my self (and many others) as Divine Raptures, Powerfully captivating all our unruly Faculties and Affections.' (*Thomas Mace*, 1676)

'I believe that music must, first and foremost, stir the heart.' (*C. P. E. Bach*, 1753)

So you must cultivate your sensibility; you must learn to be stirred by music; and you must not suppress your musically-aroused emotions. A musician cannot stir his audience unless he is stirred himself.

Today this may sound strange, but it may be that our capacity to appreciate music has been partially suppressed by the crudity of the emotion which we hear (or rather, half-hear) from the 'pop' world, where the aim seems to be to dull individual sensibilities and to substitute herd-emotion.

There is, however, a difference between the quality of emotion required at different periods. Elizabethans often (but not always) preferred their emotions raw and unrestrained. Though able to appreciate the most delicate sentiments, they could respond also to such works as *Tamburlaine*, *Lear* and *Vittoria Corombona*. Simplicity and beauty were always there, but when their emotions were aroused, they expected the maximum effect.

The eighteenth century expected as much emotion, but sought to tame it and bring it under control. Elegance was of overriding importance. The nineteenth century wanted a surface of restraint and self-control. But in their different ways, they both valued emotion and wanted music to stir their feelings as much as possible. It is a tribute to the eighteenth-century composers that the greatest of them were said to be able to balance passion and serenity at a high level of intensity.

Execution: general rules

There are certain rules that are almost standard up to about the nineteenth century.

(1) The written music did not represent what was actually played, nor was it intended to do so. Ornamentation gave spontaneity to the performance, and some of the parts were expected to be greatly changed within the harmonic limits given.

(2) The most admired form of music was singing, and instrumental pieces should be phrased and delivered as a singer would do. Some of the masters suggest that, when in doubt, you should sing over the doubtful passage and follow the phrasing and expression that would be used by a good singer.

(3) Good execution should be true and distinct; every note should be heard.

(4) Alterations required by custom and convention were not mechanical; they were governed by the character of the music and the performer's taste, as well as by the character of the hall and the audience.

(5) Paraphrasing J. J. Quantz, writing in 1752, execution is poor if the playing is feeble, indistinct, boring or coarse, and if it is in the least bit inaccurate or hurried. The aim was to interest and to arouse the listener.

(6) All fast playing must be clear and distinct.

(7) In order to appreciate and perform music well, you must hear the best, and make a conscious effort to understand *why* it is the best.

(8) Do not confuse mechanical ability with musical ability, but remember that mistakes diminish the effect on the listener.

(9) A performer was not expected to rely too much upon the written part, because he would lose the freshness and immediacy produced by improvisation and spontaneous expression.

(10) The language of the directions could indicate the style of the performance which was required. Italian style was emotional and had great vitality. French style was easy and smooth, not over-ornamented, with strong rhythm and double-dotting, and with scale passages delayed and taken fast.

There was, therefore, no exact performance; each player would suit his style, his ornaments, and his interpretation to the audience, the acoustics of the room, his own feelings, and the requirements of the occasion, but the framework of the music remained unaltered. The player was expected to adorn, to point, and to interpret, but within the framework of the composer's intentions.

For further information, you must read some of the books mentioned on pages 160–161; but for the greater part of the details which will govern your interpretation, you must look inside yourself, and examine your feelings and intentions; this is where true music comes from. Don't imagine that your interpretation is good just because it is yours; it will be good only if you have prepared yourself by listening to great players, by learning what you should know, by thinking deeply about details, and by the experience of trying out your ideas and observing their effects.

SECTION 6

21 Notation and Rudiments of Music

If you are not familiar with music, I strongly recommend that
you study these few pages. A knowledge of the basic grammar of
music and of elementary harmony will make learning the recorder
easier, and improve your playing. If you want to go further,
consult the Further Reading list.

Note lengths

A written note is a measure of duration, but the duration is
relative, not absolute. A minim (Fig. 78) is always twice the
length of a crotchet (Fig. 79) but a minim in one piece may not
be twice the length of a crochet in another piece. The following
table shows you the relative lengths of notes.

Fig. 78

Fig. 79

1 *breve*	=	2 *semibreves*
1 *semibreve*	=	2 *minims*
1 *minim*	=	2 *crotchets*
1 *crotchet*	=	2 *quavers*
1 *quaver*	=	2 *semi quavers*

Fig. 80

Fig. 81

Fig. 82

Fig. 83

Fig. 84

Semiquavers may be further divided in the same way, each successive halving being indicated by a further stroke in the 'beam'.

Fig. 85

Dotted notes

A dot by the side of a note increases its length by one-half.

Fig. 86

The second dot in a double-dotted note adds half the value of the first dot.

Fig. 87

Rests

A rest is also a measure of duration, but of silence, not sound.

1 *breve rest* = 2 *semibreve rests*
1 *semibreve rest* = 2 *minim rests*
1 *minim rest* = 2 *crotchet rests*
1 *crotchet rest* = 2 *quaver rests*

Fig. 88

Fig. 89

Fig. 90

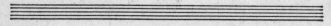

Fig. 91

Smaller rests are indicated by adding a stroke or strokes to the beam, as with notes. Rests may be dotted in the same ways as notes.

The stave

Music is written on a five-lined stave.

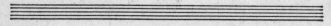

Fig. 92

Notes are given letter-names (and pitches) according to the position of the head (the oval part) on the stave, and may be placed in a space or on a line. All these notes are at the same pitch, and have the same letter-name.

Fig. 93

Clef signs

Pitch and letter-name are defined by the clef-sign which is placed at the beginning of each stave. There are three clef-signs in use today, one of which (the C clef) is moveable.

The treble-clef sign marks out G
The bass clef sign marks out F
The C clef marks out (middle) C,
    and is used as either the Alto or Tenor clef

Fig. 94

In older music you may find the clef-signs in other places, but they still mark out the same notes.

The musical alphabet

The musical alphabet is ABCDEFG. When you go past either end, the same letters are used in the same order—ABCDEFG-ABCDEFG. Notice that you also have to know the alphabet backwards—A is the lowest note in the alphabet. When applying the alphabet to the stave, line and space are used alternately:

Fig. 95

The stave may be extended by what are called 'leger-' or 'ledger'-lines.

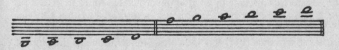

Fig. 96

A note written on the stave will have a different letter-name (and pitch) according to the clef-sign that precedes it.

Fig. 97

When treble and bass clefs are used together, as in keyboard music, the C on the leger line between the staves is called Middle C.

Fig. 98

Accidentals

The smallest interval that we write in music is called a semitone, and two semitones make one tone. If we write out the musical alphabet in order, there are tones between some of the notes and semitones between others:

$$A * B C * D * E F * G * A$$

The asterisks indicate those intervals which are tones.

Since a tone has two semitones, a note can be written between all notes that are a tone apart.

A sharp sign (Fig. 99) indicates one semitone higher, a flat sign (Fig. 100) one semitone lower, and a natural sign (Fig. 101) is used to cancel either a flat or a sharp.

♯

Fig. 99

♭

Fig. 100

♮

Fig. 101

A complete list of all the notes that could be played between A and A¹ (page 16) could be written thus:

A, A sharp, B, C, C sharp, D, D sharp, E, F, F sharp, G, G sharp, A

or, using the correct symbols,

A A♯ B C C♯ D D♯ E F F♯ G G♯ A

Fig. 102

Here we have used sharps only, and we could have used flats:

A, B flat, B, C, D flat, D, E flat, E, F, G flat, G, A flat, A

or,

A B♭ B C D♭ D E♭ E F G♭ G A♭ A

Fig. 103

In other words, notes may have two or more names.

A A♯ B C C♯ D D♯ E F F♯ G G♯ A
A B♭ B C D♭ D E♭ E F G♭ G A♭ A

Fig. 104

This is further complicated because notes can be called double-sharp (Fig. 105) or double-flat (Fig. 106) where the interval is two semitones.

𝄪   Double-sharp

Fig. 105

♭♭   Double-flat

Fig. 106

Thus, A could be called G double-sharp or B double-flat, and F may be called E sharp or G double-flat. There are good reasons for this, which can be found in Chapter 22 or in any text-book of harmony.

Pulse

In the West we are accustomed to a regular accent, both in music and in speech. English speakers tend to accent first syllables. If we say 'London, London', we tend to accent the first syllable, as we do with 'Canada, Canada'. If we read simple poetry, we make regular stresses:

> *Lón*don   *Cán*ada
> *Báa*, baa, *bláck* sheep,
> *Háve* you any *wóol*?

The accents that we make in music seem so natural that we tend to find music unusual if the stresses are differently placed.

Bar lines

In order to avoid overloading our music with stress-marks, we use bar-lines. These are vertical lines drawn across the stave (Fig. 107) and it is understood that the first note after each bar-line should be stressed. A double-bar-line (Fig. 108) indicates the end of a piece, or of an important section, or warns of a coming change of key-signature or time-signature.

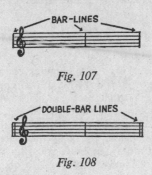

Fig. 107

Fig. 108

Time-signatures

Musicians and composers understand this implied stressing, and use the system to indicate which stresses they want. The tune in Fig. 109, written unbarred and without time-signature, would lead to differences of opinion in playing, since it can be stressed in a number of different places; but once we put in the bar-lines and time-signature (Fig. 110), all musicians will play it sufficiently alike to make performance possible; and since it can be made even more effective by extra stresses, these can also be written in (Fig. 111).

PHALÈSE. BAYERISCHE STAATS–BIBLIOTHEK.

Fig. 109

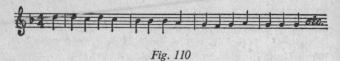

Fig. 110

Fig. 111

A time-signature consists of two figures, one above the other. The upper number tells you the number of units in a bar, and the lower figure the length of each unit. Each bar must add up to the correct length, except that where a piece begins with less than a full bar, the last bar is normally written to make up the correct amount. The lower figures are really fractions of a semibreve: a lower figure of 1 means semibreve units, 2 means minim units, 4, crotchet units, 8, quaver units, and so on. Notice that the lower figure is always even; there is no way of expressing any other fractions of a semibreve in time-signatures.

$\dfrac{2}{1}$ = two semibreves' worth of notes in every bar

$\dfrac{2}{2}$ = two minims' worth of notes in every bar

$\dfrac{3}{2}$ = three minims' worth of notes in every bar

$\dfrac{2}{4}$ = two crotchets' worth of notes in every bar

$\dfrac{2}{8}$ = two quavers' worth of notes in every bar

The upper figure of a time-signature may be odd or even.

Repeats

A composer may want you to play a piece or a section of a piece more than once. He indicates this by putting two dots against the middle of the stave (usually with a double-bar) at the beginning of a section, and two dots with a double-bar at the place from which he wants you to go back. Four dots are sometimes used.

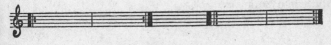

Fig. 112

When you play a section twice and the composer wants a different ending the second time, he uses what are called 'first-time' and 'second-time' bars.

Fig. 113

For the first time through, you play to the end of the bar marked 1 (notice the repeat-mark at the double-bar) and go back to the beginning; at the end of the repeat you play the bar marked 2 instead of the bar marked 1.

There are also some words which indicate repeats.

Da Capo: Go back to the beginning.
Da Capo al Fine: Go back to the beginning and stop when you come to the word *Fine*.
Dal Segno: Go back to the sign and repeat from there.

There are many different signs in use, but Fig. 114 shows the most common.

Fig. 114

Duplets, triplets etc.

Where the composer wants to write a group of notes which do not fit the rhythmic pattern set by the time-signature, he writes a figure above the group (which gives the number of the notes in this group) and—usually—joins them by a slur. They must be fitted into the time available.

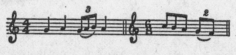

Fig. 115

Grouping

When music is written or printed, the notes are grouped so that the accents or divisions of the bar are made clearer.

Fig. 116

Signs

There are some signs which are used to indicate that a note or notes should be played differently. The main ones are:

Accent | — ∨ v ≻ *etc.*

Fig. 117

Staccato
The note is to be played shorter than its written length.

Fig. 118

Pause
Play this note longer than its written length.

Fig. 119

Slur
These notes are to be joined together —i.e. for wind-players, only the first note is to be tongued and the others follow without tonguing.

Fig. 120

Key-signatures

Whether it is because we are conditioned or because it is instinctive, we tend to use certain relationships of notes, called 'keys' (see Chapter 22). Composers use different keys to produce different musical effects, and they will indicate this in the music by writing a key-signature at the beginning of a piece, and by changing this where they think it necessary. The key-signature is the group of sharps or flats written at the beginning of a stave, after the clef-sign.

In a sense, key-signatures are not necessary; the same effect could be obtained by writing a sharp or flat in front of each note affected; but this would make music much harder to read; so one practical effect of a key-signature is to inform the player that each time a certain note is written it must be sharpened or flattened. With the key-signature in Fig. 121 every F in the piece must be sharpened; and in Fig. 122 every B must be flattened.

Fig. 121

Fig. 122

Key-signatures can contain up to seven sharps or flats (one key has neither sharps nor flats in its key-signature) and these are always written in the same order, to make reading easier. So there is no need (normally) to take time to identify each sharp or flat; a key-signature of three sharps means that all F's, C's, and G's must be sharpened. The exception to the pattern is a seven-sharp key-signature which should be written as in Fig. 123; in order to save space and avoid leger-lines, it is always written as in Fig. 124. On occasion, a six-sharp key-signature is similarly changed.

Fig. 123

Fig. 124

A seven-flat key-signature is written like this:

Fig. 125

As time goes on, you will become acquainted with all key-signatures you are likely to meet—recorder-players seldom meet more than three sharps or three flats. All the key-signatures, and also a quick method of working out keys from key-signatures are given in Chapter 22.

Accidentals

A composer may want to move out of the scale-pattern he has started with, and to show that a particular note should be sharpened or flattened. He does this by putting the correct symbol in front of the note.

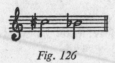

Fig. 126

This temporary alteration lasts only for the bar in which it is written, and does not start until the accidental is reached. Should a composer want to cancel the accidental before the end of the bar is reached, he uses a natural sign:

Fig. 127

All three signs may be used as reminders, in which case they are normally bracketed (Fig. 128), and in music which has been edited, accidentals which the editor thinks are necessary but are not in the original are placed over the note.

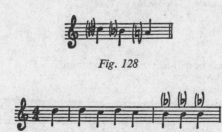

Fig. 128

Fig. 129

22 Elementary Harmony

Some knowledge of harmony is essential to a musician. Basic information is given here; if you want to go further, see Chapter 25 and the Further Reading list.

Scales

There are two kinds of scales in modern use: diatonic and chromatic. The diatonic scale consists of tones and semitones; the chromatic scale entirely of semitones. The diatonic scale is composed of eight notes, and the interval from the lowest note to the highest is called an octave (intervals are always measured from the lower note). Each note in the scale has a number and technical name, referring to its relative position in the scale.

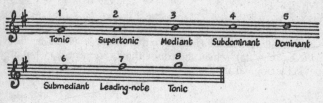

Fig. 130

A scale may be divided into two tetrachords:

Fig. 131

Intervals

If you number the notes in a scale from the bottom upwards, then the distances between the lowest note and any other are named as follows:

From 1 *to* 1 = a unison   *From* 1 *to* 6 = a sixth
    1 *to* 2 = a second   1 *to* 7 = a seventh
    1 *to* 3 = a third   1 *to* 8 = an octave
    1 *to* 4 = a fourth   1 *to* 9 = a ninth
    1 *to* 5 = a fifth

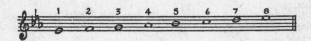

Fig. 132

—and so on. These names can be qualified by the addition of major, minor, perfect, augmented and diminished (for example, A to C natural is a minor third), but the interval between letter-names will always give you the right *number* of the interval; thus (and try it on your recorder), F double sharp to G double flat is a second.

Construction of scales

There are two main divisions of diatonic scales, major and minor, and they differ in the pattern of tones and semitones which they contain. The major scale, from the bottom upwards, has tone, tone, semitone, tone, tone, tone, semitone.

Fig. 133

There are two main types of minor scale; in the melodic minor the pattern going upwards is tone, semitone, tone, tone, tone, tone, semitone; and, going downwards, tone, tone, semitone, tone, tone, semitone, tone.

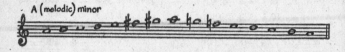

A (melodic) minor

Fig. 134

In the harmonic minor scale the intervals, both upwards and downwards, are tone, semitone, tone, tone, semitone, tone-and-a-half, semitone.

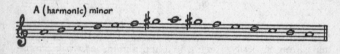

A (harmonic) minor

Fig. 135

Other patterns of scale exist, but these are the most usual.

Recognising key-signatures

Key-signatures are set at the beginning of every line of music, and are composed of either sharps or flats. No more than seven sharps or seven flats are used, and these are always written in the same order, for ease of recognition.

You will memorise many of these, but there is a simple set of rules which will help you to work out the key from the key-signature. For major sharp keys, find the note one semitone higher than the last sharp; this will give you the key-note (the name of the key). For major flat keys, look at the last flat but one; this is the key-note. The rules do not work for C major, which has no key-signature, nor for F major, which has one flat.

Fig. 136

To work out minor keys, identify the key as a major key, and count three semitones down. The relative minor to C major is A minor.

Modulations

A composer may want to move into another key, which he does either by putting in a double-bar and a fresh key-signature or by adding accidentals. Thus, if you are playing in D major and find a G sharp accidental, you will be playing either in A major or in F sharp minor. It is important to notice when this happens because of the changes of intonation that are required (see Chapter 18).

Why are keys necessary

Beginners sometimes wonder why all music could not be written in C with occasional accidentals. One reason for the existence of keys is that many accidentals would make reading more difficult; another is that the sound of music played in different keys is different. Almost all instruments produce a different quality of sound in different parts of their range.

Transposition

You may have noticed a little sign at the beginning of descant parts:

Fig. 137

This means that the music is to be played an octave higher than it is written; if it is placed under the stave it means an octave lower. This is usually done to save space between staves and to avoid the confusion that could be produced by many leger-lines. So the descant, sopranino and bass recorders are known as 'transposing instruments', and there are also others (the clarinet, for instance).

Transposition is not always made at the octave; you may need to transpose music into other keys, particularly if you are going to adapt music for recorders.

When you write transposed music, first work out what the new key will be, and put in the new key-signature. Then write in the notes, keeping the correct intervals. Be careful over accidentals; work out what they should be in the new key. The only real difficulty in transposition is in keeping up your concentration.

Triads

These are three-note chords, spaced in thirds. In any scale you can build triads on each note, like this:

Fig. 138

Notice that if the lowest note is on a line, both the others are on lines; if the lowest note is in a space, both the others are in spaces.

Of these triads (they are always referred to by Roman numbers), I, IV, and V are the most important harmonically, since they contain between them all the notes of the scale.

Fig. 139

You can harmonise a simple tune using these three chords only, but it will be simple harmony and not particularly interesting. If you examine the bass lines of folk or pop music, you will see how much of it is built up from triads.

Inversions

A triad is still a triad as long as it contains the same three notes. Thus triad I in C major can be written in three ways; and this applies to all triads.

Root position   1st inversion   2nd inversion

Fig. 140

Cadences

There are some chord-sequences that seem right at the end of a sentence of music. The two that give the greatest sense of finality are the Perfect Cadence (triad V to triad I)

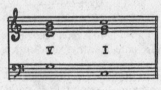

Fig. 141

and the Plagal Cadence (triad IV to triad I).

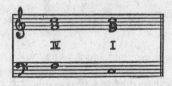

Fig. 142

There are also the Imperfect Cadence (I–IV, II–IV, VI–V, or IV–V) and the Interrupted or Surprise Cadence (V–VI).

Try to train your ears to hear cadences; it will help you in phrasing and in effective performance.

23 Performance

Sooner or later you will want to perform in public, whether with an accompanist or in consort; I think it is right that you should, provided that you can do justice to yourself and to the music that you choose.

Unfortunately, opportunities to perform in public are usually rare and have to be made.

Opportunities

As an unknown soloist or group, you will not have any drawing power for audiences. Therefore, when you are ready to perform, you need to be in touch with some organisation which will provide a ready-made audience—people who are in the habit of meeting together regularly, and who want entertainment as a part of their evening.

There are many such bodies. Ask at your town information centre, and you will be provided with a list of clubs and other organised bodies. Between them they want a good deal of cultural activity, and they will be interested in finding something new and different. You will probably have to wait, as they normally book a year ahead; but this will give you time to prepare.

Unfortunately, there are likely to be one or two problems. In the first place, most of them are not prepared to pay. A few will offer expenses, some may offer a fee, but when the fee and expenses are spread over rehearsal time, equipment, music and travelling, you are guaranteed to make a loss. As a professional, I resent the system that encourages amateurs to take the jobs I should have had, and which encourages customers to think that music is free; as an ex-amateur, I realise that only amateurs have a chance of reaching these audiences, and perhaps preparing the way for a professional concert later.

In addition, these bodies often have little idea of what is

required: frequently the keyboard instrument, if there is one, is defective or incorrectly tuned; and they seldom think of providing adequate light. So examine their piano beforehand, and be prepared either to do without or to bring your own keyboard instrument.

In order to get bookings, you must be known. In order to be known, you must get bookings. This is the normal situation, and comparatively few break out of the vicious circle. Try to get an interview with your local paper, or radio station, or television. They are always looking for new material for the news and magazine programmes. But (*a*) they will not pay a fee (though expenses can sometimes be claimed) and (*b*), if you are going to profit by a television or radio appearance, you must be good enough. Most television interviews require only a snippet of music, so choose something attractive that you can do well, and rehearse it thoroughly.

Festivals

One way of making a reputation is to do well at music festivals, whether competitive or non-competitive, for here you can have a public performance (and a criticism by a professional musician) for, what is normally a small entry fee. You can enter at any level—classes usually range from beginners' to advanced—and enter more advanced classes as your abilities develop; many soloists have gone this way. Children form the majority of entrants but festivals are not restricted to children and standards of playing can be remarkably high.

Rehearsal

On the platform, there should be no mistakes; and if they do occur, they must be compensated for immediately. Rehearse your programme under concert conditions several times, never stopping unless there is total chaos. And never perform a piece until everybody is quite sure what is going to happen.

Make sure that all copies are properly marked with details of interpretation and programme, and even such obvious things as the repeats that are not going to be made. Under the stress of performance, people can forget even very familiar details.

Tuning

Recorder players should tune up beforehand, but it is a useless exercise unless it is a real attempt to get a common intonation and maintain it. Also, your recorders should be warmed up to the same extent before you tune. It is often a good idea to play something together before you come on stage; but don't play for too long, and make sure that the audience cannot hear you.

If any players are going to change recorders during the programme, these too must be warmed up. Men can leave the head of the instrument in an inside pocket, but ladies are not always able to do this. I have heard of a hot-water-bottle in a wooden frame being used, but this needs experimenting with beforehand.

Costume

To a real musician the conditions, the appearance of the players, the organisation of the concert, are not important. What matters is the music. But for most audiences they *do* matter; I have known cases where uncomfortable conditions have ruined a concert for the audience.

You must do everything you can to 'sell' yourself and to make your performance attractive.

Personal appearance matters. If you wear period costume, wear it with conviction.

If you are not going to wear costume, then uniformity of style does improve appearance. A body of players, in my opinion, looks best in evening dress. If you have made the effort to prepare a concert, you should reflect this by dressing as well as you can.

Platform manners

A bow is the accepted form of greeting and farewell from performers, but it should be well done, and done together.

You should look interested in what you are doing. A player who has a long rest, or who has to sit out for a movement, should sit still and listen attentively to the others. Where a player is not required for a piece of reasonable length, he should leave the platform, if possible.

Be as efficient and tidy on the platform as you can. The audience is looking as well as listening, and clutter and fuss distract their attention.

Disasters

They do happen, even in the best of circles. Instruments break down; music gets lost; a player fails to turn up. Make the most careful preparations you can; cover up, if possible. If you can't, apologise to the audience and get on with the job as best you can.

Programme

With recorders, contrast is the thing. Alternate your numbers; after a solo, play a consort; follow sixteenth-century music by modern. Make a change of pace. But don't arrange things in such a way that people have to enter and leave the platform every minute. Always assume that your audience will easily be bored.

Leading

The leader has a difficult, very important, and rewarding job. He must know his music well, be able to cue people in for their entries, help them to recover if they get lost, set and keep correct tempi, and make clean entries and good endings. When he is also playing himself, this is difficult; but it has to be done.

Obviously he should be playing from full score, unless turning over is too difficult; and equally obviously, all the other players must watch him.

Give the job to your best musician, unless he is temperamentally unqualified to lead, and make sure that all the players know what he is going to do and how he is going to do it. The less obvious his indications have to be, the better.

Accompanists

Most solos should be accompanied, and if you do not have a keyboard player or keyboard instrument, consider a guitarist or lutenist, or even percussion. The accompanist has to support and amplify the soloist's intentions, to keep with him, no matter how much the soloist deviates from what they have arranged, and he must never outshine the soloist. Therefore, in duet work, rehearse thoroughly until you work as one unit.

Platform nerves

There is no instant, automatic cure for platform nerves. They strike when you are least expecting them and they can be devastating. The surest thing is to be very well-prepared, but the following points can help.

First, you must like what you are doing; you must like your audience and be genuinely trying to communicate to them what you are feeling about your music. It is better if you really feel this, but in any case try to convince yourself that it is true.

Secondly, try to find out what state of mind makes you fittest to perform, and cultivate it. Some prefer to be busy, others want to feel calm. And think of others; avoid worrying other performers before their entrance.

To some extent you must take yourself out of the picture. Don't think of the evening as a showcase for yourself; you are there to interpret the composer to the audience, and the music matters much more than you do. To worry beforehand is natural; but if you take your worries to the platform you will play badly.

You may well find that a deep breath or two just before your entry is helpful.

Instruments

There is little that can go wrong with a recorder, but things do happen. Always examine your instruments before you enter to reassure yourself that all is well.

If your recorder is too wet, swab out the bore and clean the windway with something absorbent. The pad of your key can be dried with a cigarette-paper and the spring mended with a rubber band.

It is always good to have a spare instrument.

Turning over

Most publishers arrange their printing so that there is time for the performer to turn over and begin or end a page with rests. But this does not always happen, and if you are playing from a score, it is unusual. Turn up the bottom right-hand corners of the music so that you can turn quickly. Where necessary, have two copies, or write out a few bars which will allow you to turn at a reasonable place and stick them to the copy. If you happen to be sitting two to a stand, the inside player always does the turning.

Beginnings and endings

These must be clean and accurate. A small signal from the leader is enough, but it will take practice to make sure that you are together.

Organisation

A concert needs organising. Someone must decide times, transport, equipment, dress, and so on, and see that the other players know what they have to know.

Care of the music is important. It is best if one person takes charge of all the concert music, sees that the marks are put into all copies, that the music is all present and in order, and puts the parts into a separate folder for each player.

Timing

It is possible to time each of your pieces beforehand, and add the times up, but you cannot be sure how much time will be spent between items. As a rough guide, a two-hour concert with an interval will need one hour's playing time. You can prepare a couple of optional pieces if you wish, but it is better to leave the audience wanting more than to play for too long.

Programmes

It is becoming more and more expensive to produce a paper programme, and many people now rely on announcements.

If you do have a paper programme, space it out as attractively as you can, and keep the language simple and interesting. If you can find some interesting facts about the music or the composers, use them. *Grove's Dictionary of Music and Musicians* is a good source.

24 Opportunities to Learn

Whatever country you live in, there are opportunities to learn and to play the recorder, but it is not always easy for a solitary player to find out about them. Once you are a member of the recorder-playing community, information is passed around; so the first thing to do is to contact other players.

Information

The music-teacher in your local school is likely to be a good source of information; at the very least, he or she can tell you where to enquire further. It is also probable that higher levels in the educational system have even more information, once you can get in touch with the appropriate department. Organisations are different in different countries, but you should find the following helpful:

U.S.A.: Try the State Education Departments; the Institute of International Education, 809 United Nations Plaza, New York, N.Y. 10017 publishes a list (for foreign students) of summer programmes in the U.S.A.

Canada: The local Board of Education or the Ministry or Provincial Department of Education.

Australia: The State or Federal Department of Education.

New Zealand: The Director General of Education, Dept. Education Private Bag, Wellington.

South Africa: The South African College of Music, University of Capetown, Randebosch, Cape Town 7700.

U.K.: The County Education Departments.

India: The Academy of Dance, Music, and Drama, The Sangett Napak Akademi, Rabindra Bhavan, 35 Feroze Shah Road, New Delhi.

Many countries have national recorder societies and you should enquire about there.

Other organisations

The Dolmetsch Foundation, c/o Messrs. Arnold Dolmetsch, Kings Road, Haslemere, Surrey, GU27 2QJ, U.K. is international, and publishes a list of all its members.

The British Council publishes a list of courses in summer schools in the U.K.

Publications

This is a rapidly-changing field, and you would probably be best advised to read whatever music magazines you can find, looking for advertisements. Consult your local music shop for advice.

In the U.S.A. *The American Recorder* is useful, and there are several publications in Germany, of which *Der Blockflöten Spiegel* and *Die Zeitschrift für Hausmusik* are the best known.

The Strad, which is published internationally, sometimes has information, and the Oxford University Press in Britain produces *Early Music*, a most valuable quarterly, which is available in other countries.

Examinations

I strongly urge you, if you wish to take the recorder seriously, to prepare for and to sit some of the examinations in music. This gives you a target to aim at, and a course in music as well as in recorder-playing (there are both theoretical and practical examinations) which can be immensely useful to you. Moreover, entering for an examination tends to keep you working. You might even end up with letters after your name!

Trinity College of Music, Manderville Place, London W1M 6AQ, conducts examinations in recorder-playing in local centres on a national and international scale in the U.K., the U.S.A., and other countries. The syllabus is obtainable from the College and from their international branches. At the moment there are six grades for which you can be examined (1, 2, 4, 5, 6, and 8), and these will give you a wide musical education as well as practical tests.

In the U.K. The Guildhall School of Music, London, offers external examinations (Grades 2, 4, 6, and 8 for recorder-players).

The Associated Board of the Royal Schools of Music, 14 Bedford Square, London WC1B 3JG conducts examinations in many parts of the world, but not, unfortunately, in the U.S.A. They do not examine in recorder-playing, but I strongly recommend their examinations (graded) on the theory of music, for which they also have some excellent preparatory books.

Also, find out about diplomas and degrees in music particular to your own country.

Evening classes

These offer you a great opportunity to learn from a qualified musician and to make music with others.

In Britain, you can find out whether there are such classes from the local evening-school organisation (many produce lists of courses in the autumn), or from the County Education Office (ask for the Music Organiser). If there do not seem to be any relevant classes, the County will probably provide one if you can assure them of adequate support.

If and when you find such a class, remember that, in most areas, you need a certain number of students to start, and that the class will be cancelled if attendance drops below a minimum figure. Also, you will probably be asked to buy some music.

Don't expect more individual attention than your teacher can give; other students have claims on him too. Use every opportunity to learn; talk and listen to the others, observe what they do and why they do it, and make good use of your practice time at home.

Summer schools

These are an international institution, and attending one can be a wonderful experience. Spending a week or a fortnight in an atmosphere that is solely concerned with music, mixing with professional players, working day and night to improve your standards, often in very pleasant surroundings, is immensely worth while, and I recommend you to try it at least once.

Not all schools offer recorder courses, but in Britain and the U.S.A. at least there are special recorder summer schools. Their advertisements will appear in some of the publications recommended in the early part of this chapter.

The schools will send brochures to you if you enquire and you should study their information carefully when picking a course. Some schools offer beginners' and intermediate courses; try not to land yourself on a course where the standard is too high for you. Summer schools are very helpful and kind—they want you to come back—but if you get a feeling of inferiority, whether justified or not, you will not be happy.

Go prepared to enjoy yourself. Most schools allow generous time between classes, and playing during this period is optional. You may take the time off, or play all the time, if you wish; but you will be well-advised to rest from playing some part of the time.

Don't expect any immediate great improvement. If you spend all the time playing, as many do, you may well be playing more badly at the end of your time than you did at the beginning because you will be so thoroughly tired; but over the next six months or so you will find that you have learnt much more than you realised.

25 Acquiring a Repertoire

As you learn, you will get to know a stock of music: your own, your friends', music that you have borrowed, and so on. But so much recorder music is published that you are unlikely to see it all. Moreover, the publishing trade is changing rapidly, and many pieces are not reprinted as stocks run out.

Your music-shop may well have a stock of recorder-music, but it is unlikely to be extensive. However, they will have publishers' catalogues, and at the worst, you can write to the publishers yourself; this means that you may be choosing blindly, unless the publishers allow sale or return.

Summer Schools and other courses often have a stock of publications; and there are sometimes Trade Fairs and exhibitions which you can visit.

Second-hand music

In many countries it is possible to buy music second-hand, and there are even specialists in second-hand music. They may not, of course, have recorder music at the particular moment you want it, but many issue catalogues. Second-hand bookshops also may stock music.

Foyles Book Shop in the Charing Cross Road, London, has a large stock of music, some of it second-hand, and I have bought from Holleyman and Treacher, 21a/22 Duke Street, Brighton, and from Galliard, London. Booths, in Hay-on-Wye, bill themselves as the biggest second-hand bookshop in the world, and they have a music section. Write to The Hay Music Shop, 2 Lion Street, Hay-on-Wye.

Specialist shops

The increased interest in early music has produced a number of specialist shops and specialist publishers in several countries. Their names and addresses are best found from the specialist magazines, of which several exist. Ask your music shop about them.

Borrowing

Most public libraries have books of music which can be borrowed.

Sources

If you want to find some rare music, try some of the big reference libraries—for instance, the British Library in London, or the Library of Congress in the U.S.A. University libraries can also be useful. When you do find something you want, there is no need to waste time hand-copying it; all big libraries have reproduction facilities, and their charges are not usually very heavy. Scholarly books often have lists of sources, and sometimes even give the library and reference number, so that you can write to a library asking for a microfilm or other copy of what you want.

Original music

If you really want something that can be yours alone, try looking for a composer. Many teachers of music have had training in composition, and some of them may be eager to have their compositions played. You may have to explain the characteristics of recorders, and to specify the type of music you would like, but you will often get a pleased response; there is much talent lying idle.

Copying

Many people copy out music, either by hand or by machine, but do be careful over copyright. The legal details of copyright differ in different countries, but in the U.K. copyright exists for many years after the death of an author, and it is a legal offence to copy even one bar of a copyright piece. Moreover, you will be reducing the composer's income, which is frequently small.

26 The Recorder Today

It is not known how many people play the recorder today, but there are certainly recorder-players in every country. The instrument is very popular in schools and you will find recorder teachers in music colleges and other places where there is high-level musical instruction.

However, it has not yet gained widespread acceptance among professional musicians as an instrument for performance. Though there are professional recorder-players, and some real virtuosi among them, there are not many professional opportunities for recorder-players. This is partly because the recorder is too light in tone compared with modern instruments, even though there are players who can perform successfully against a modern orchestra.

But the recorder is a musical instrument; it can be as much a life-study as any other, and even the best players have not yet reached its limits. The fact that it is not, in general, as loud as a modern instrument is not necessarily a drawback. A consort of recorders, particularly, has an individual sound that no other combination of instruments possesses. Pepys' ravishment at the sound of a consort—('which was so sweet that it ravished me, and indeed, in a word, did so wrap up my soul that it made me really sick, just as I have formerly been when in bed with my wife . . . so as I could not believe that ever any music hath that real command over the soul of a man as this did upon me')—is an indication of the effect that recorder music can have upon people of sensibility.

The increasing popularity of early music must mean that standards of recorder-playing will improve, and that there will be increased opportunities for professionals, just as the increasing numbers of manufacturers of early instruments should mean that there will be better recorders.

At school level, I think the recorder will remain popular, particularly in junior schools. It has enlarged the scope of school music courses, and it has encouraged many children to go on to orchestral instruments. Indeed, there may be some connection between the enthusiasm for the recorder and the growth of instrumental teaching in schools.

But it is in the amateur movement that the recorder has had its greatest success. People the world over have found an outlet in the recorder for their desire to make music, and there is first-class amateur recorder-playing in most countries of the world. It has opened up new opportunities and brought pleasure to millions.

Further Reading and Sources of Information

If you join the Dolmetsch Foundation, you will have access to their list of members, which is world-wide, as well as to their publications, which contain much information. Write to Arnold Dolmetsch Ltd., King's Road, Haslemere, Surrey, England.

Early Music (Oxford University Press) will give you a number of names and addresses of people who are active in the recorder world, as well as publishers and makers of instruments.

Your choice of books will be governed by your taste and inclinations, but I offer here a list of books which I own, use, and have found helpful. All are currently available internationally.

Musicology, performance and so on

Arnold Dolmetsch: *The Interpretation of the Music of the XVI and XVII Centuries*, Oxford University Press, 1946 (repr.)

Robert Donington: *The Interpretation of Early Music*, Faber & Faber, 1974

Friedrich Blume: *Renaissance and Baroque Music*, Faber & Faber, 1967

J. P. Rameau: *Treatise on Harmony* (tr. Gosset) Dover, 1971

Ornithoparcus & Dowland: *A Compendium of Musical Practice*, Dover, 1973

T. Morley: *A Plain and Easy Introduction to Practical Music*, Dent, 1952

C. P. E. Bach: *Essay on the True Art of Playing Keyboard Instruments*, Eulenberg, 1974

T. Mace: *Music's Monument*, Editions du Centre National de la Recherche Scientifique, 1958

Recorders

H. Peter: *The Recorder, Its Traditions and Tasks*, Hinrichsen, 1958

A. Rowland-Jones: *Recorder Technique*, Oxford University Press, 1959
E. Hunt: *The Recorder and its Music*, Herbert Jenkins, 1962

Psychology

C. E. Seashore: *Psychology of Music*, Dover, 1967
P. Buck: *Psychology for Musicians*, Oxford University Press, 1956

History

A. Baines: *Woodwind Instruments and their History*, Faber & Faber, 1943 (repr.)

Physics of music

A. Wood: *The Physics of Music*, Methuen, 1962
G. Russell-Smith: *Sound Sense*, Boosey & Hawkes, 1967

Harmony

Elementary: *The associated Board series of Questions and Exercises*
Rudiments and Theory of Music
Both are published by The Associated Board of the Royal Schools of Music, 14 Bedford Square, London WC1B 3JG.
More advanced: *Commonsense Harmony*, Mills Music, 1967

General

Grove's Dictionary of Music and Musicians (Macmillan).
Exercises: I can thoroughly recommend both Margaret and Robert Donington's *Scales, Exercises and Arpeggios for the Recorder* (Oxford University Press) and H. U. Staeps *Tägliche Pensum* (Universal).
Dance: Mabel Dolmetsch's books on dancing (Routledge and Kegan Paul); also Gregg Universal Press publish a series of reprints of famous books on period dancing.

Glossary

This Glossary gives the definitions of the commoner musical terms connected with recorder-playing. If the definition you are seeking is not here, try a musical dictionary, any text-book on music, or any book on the technical aspects of music.

Accelerando Getting faster

Acciaccatura A 'crushed note'; a very short note played immediately before a note in the text

Accidental A flat, sharp, or natural inserted in the music, as distinct from a key-signature

Adagio At ease

Agitato Agitated

Alla In the style of

Allargando Broadening

Allegro A fastish marching speed, MM 152–184

Altblockflöte A treble recorder

Alternative fingerings Non-standard fingerings which nevertheless can give a correctly-pitched note

Alto recorder A treble recorder

Andante A moderate walking-pace, MM 126–152

Animato Lively

Aperture Sometimes used to mean 'finger-hole'

Appoggiatura An ornamental grace-note, longer than an acciaccatura

Arpeggio A series of connected notes, usually belonging to a chord. Lit., 'harp-like'

Articulation Tonguing and phrasing

Ascending Moving upwards in pitch

A tempo Resume normal speed

Atonal Not in any definite key

Baroque In a certain style, usually '18th century'

Beading A semi-ornamental moulding on a recorder, usually designed to strengthen the joint

Beak The mouthpiece of a recorder

Beak-flute A recorder

Beam The line or lines connecting the stems of two or more quavers or smaller notes

Beat The regular stress or accent usually present in music; a conductor's motions when 'beating time'; one unit of a bar

Block, *fipple* See *fipple-block*

Blockflöte A recorder

Blurring Failure to change

cleanly from one note to another

Bore The hollow tube of a recorder.

Bracket The curved bracket-line which is used to join two or more staves which are to be played at the same time

Brackets Brackets are used to indicate optional notes or accidentals, or sometimes editors' markings.

Breath-mark An indication that a small break should be made in a musical line, as if breath were being taken; a place to take breath

Brio Vigour

Broken chord A chord in which the elements are played successively, not simultaneously

Buttress-fingering A technique of fingering in which one finger is used to support the recorder for certain notes

Calando Gradually getting softer and slower.

Canon A melody which harmonises with itself, so that two or more players may play the same tune starting at different places, or may enter successively

Cantabile In a singing style

Chord Three or more notes sounded simultaneously

Chromatic Moving by semitones

Clean Accurate and neat

Clef-sign A symbol which indicates that a certain point on

the stave has a particular letter-name

Common chord A chord of three (sometimes four, the tonic being repeated) notes which includes the tonic, mediant, and dominant of a scale (1st, 3rd, 5th, or doh-me-soh)

Con With

Consort Two or (usually) more players playing together in different parts

Contrapuntal Music which moves by lines rather than by chords.

Crack Producing a note other than that which was fingered and intended, usually higher

Cracks, playing in the Being consistently out of tune

Crescendo Getting louder. Also marked

Crook Sometimes used for the pipe which leads the breath into many bass recorders

Cross-fingering A fingering to produce a note in which the fingers are not laid on consecutive holes

Cushion Sometimes used to mean the pad of the end joint of the finger; very occasionally the pad of a key

Da capo A direction to return to the beginning of the music and repeat

Decrescendo Gradually softer. Also marked

Descending Going downwards in pitch

Diminuendo Gradually softer. Also marked

———————

Diskant Blockflöte A descant recorder

Dolce Sweetly

Dominant The fifth note of the scale

Dot A dot over or under a note requires it to be detached; a dot by the side of a note lengthens it by one-half; a double-dot by the side of a note further lengthens the note by half the value of the first dot

Double holes The pairs of small holes which on some recorders are used for holes 6 and 7

Double-tonguing A device to make it easier to play faster by using alternately the tip and back of the tongue ('T–K–T–K' or 'D–G–D–G')

Duplet Two notes performed in the time of three

Dynamics Variations in volume

Ear A player's ability to distinguish fine shades of pitch; his ability to hear musical qualities

Enharmonic Having to do with harmony outside the original key

Espressivo Expressively

-etto (*as suffix*) Not so much as

Fermata A pause

Fine The end

Fipple A term of ill-defined meaning or use; possibly the arrangement (windway and knife-edge) used to produce recorder sound (see Plates 2–4). Also used on other instruments

Fipple-block The shaped block that closes the mouth end of a recorder and forms part of the windway (see Plates 2–4)

Flauto A recorder (usually treble), for part of the eighteenth century

Flauto diritto A recorder

Flauto Dolce A recorder

Flauto piccolo A sopranino recorder

Flute A recorder (usually treble), for part of the eighteenth century

Flute a bec A recorder

Flute, Beak- A recorder

Foot-joint The lowest joint of a recorder

Fork-hold A cross-fingering, q.v.

Forte (*f*) Loud

Fortepiano Loud, then soft

Fortissimo (*ff*) Very loud. More F's may be added to indicate further increases in volume

Forzando With a strong accent

Fundamental The lowest note in a chord; the lowest note (sometimes) on an instrument.

Fuoco Fire

German fingering A system of placing the holes in a recorder to give a simpler fingering

Giocoso Gay, merry

Grave Gravely

Grazioso Gracefully

Half-holing Covering half, or a portion of, a finger-hole

Harmonic An irregularity in a simple variation; a squeak.

Head (of a note) The oval portion of a written note

Head/head-joint The upper part of a recorder

Hold Sometimes used to mean 'fingering'

Imitation A musical device, in which one phrase resembles another

Improvisation Making up a tune and/or harmony while you are playing it

Interval The distance between two notes (starting with the lower)

Intonation Having to do with being in tune. Can also be used to mean 'tone'

-issimo (as suffix) Very

Joints The portions of a recorder, usually head-, middle- and foot-

Just intonation One of the many systems of relative intonation in scales

Key-signature An ordered arrangement of flats or sharps to indicate the key in which the music is to be played

Knife-edge The sharp edge which, in a recorder, splits the current of air as it emerges from the windway

Lapping The lining of a joint

Lapping-thread The thread used to form a lapping

Largo Slow and stately

Leading-note The seventh note of a scale

Leak Failure to cover a hole correctly with one or more fingers, or to seal the lips round a mouthpiece

Legato Literally, joined. A passage in which the notes are only just separated

Leggiero Lightly

Lento Very slowly

Lining Sometimes used for *Lapping*, q.v.

Lip A player's use of his lips to form and control a note; sometimes the knife-edge of a recorder

Lunga Long

Ma But

Maestoso Majestically

Marcato Marked, accented

Mediant The third note in a scale

Meno Less

Metre The regular pulsation of accent usually found in music

Mezzo Half

MM (Maelzel's metronome) An indication of speed, usually put thus:

MM $\bullet$ = 60

i.e. one crotchet per second

Moderato At moderate speed

Mordent An ornament

Morendo Dying away

Mosso Movement

Moto Movement

Mouthpiece The beak of a recorder

Natural The sign that cancels an accidental

Non Not

Notation A system of writing down information, usually musical

Octave The distance between a note and its nearest neighbour of the same letter-name

Overblowing Putting too much air in the windway. Sometimes, forcing a note up to the next harmonic by extra breath, as in playing a pinched note

Overtones Additions to the simple wave-form of sound which produces a pitched note; they give the sound its individual character

Pads The inside of the joint at the tip of a finger; small cushions, usually of leather, on the inside of a key

Part The particular line of music which a player is following; the actual paper on which it is printed

Pause Increasing the length of a note to more than its written value. There is no defined length for a pause; its duration depends on the player's judgement

Pesante Heavily

Phrasing Marking the divisions and sub-divisions of a melody

Pianissimo (*pp*) Very soft. Extra P's may be added for extra quietness.

Piano (*p*) Soft

Pinched note Any note which requires the use of the thumb-nail in the thumb-hole

Pitch The number of cycles per second required to produce a note; the height of a note above a defined base

Plu More

Poco A little

Polyphonic Literally, having many voices. Music in which the parts are independent as well as interdependent

Portamento see *Scooping*

Presto Fast. MM 184–200

Progression A sequence of chords

Pulse The system of regular stresses which occurs in most music

Quodlibet A piece of music in which several well-known (usually) melodies are blended together. Often improvised

Rallentando Gradually slower

Range The distance between the highest and lowest notes of an instrument or a piece of music

Range of recorders

SOPRANINO

DESCANT

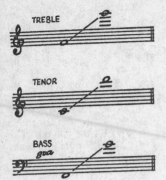

TREBLE

TENOR

BASS
8va

Register A particular portion of an instrument's range, usually one in which there is a characteristic sound, and which is often marked off by a radical change in fingering, e.g., pinched notes

Rest A measured period of silence

Resultant harmonic An unwanted extra note usually resulting from a member or members of a consort playing out of tune

Ritardando Gradually slower

Ritenuto Gradually slower

Round A tune which will harmonise with itself (see *Canon*). Sometimes rounds are repeated; canons are not

Rubato Playing in which time is taken from some notes and added to others

Scooping Making a messy join between notes of different pitches; sliding up to a note. When this is done deliberately it is called *Portamento*

Semitone The smallest interval in written music. Two semitones make one tone

Sempre Always, still

Senza Without

Shading Partially covering a hole or holes to get special effects, usually for enharmonic reasons

Shake A trill

Sixth-flute A term of doubtful meaning; often thought to be a descant recorder in D, but according to Woodcock (early eighteenth century) who wrote six concertos for it, a treble recorder in A

Snap A short note joined to a longer one

Sonority Sometimes used for 'tone'

Sopran Blockflöte Descant recorder

Soprano recorder Descant recorder

Sostenuto Sustained

Speak, to To produce a musical sound, as in 'this recorder speaks easily'

Spirito Spirit

Split thumb Sometimes used for 'pinched'

Staccato Separated, short

Stave, staff The five lines that form the frame for written music. A stave does not indicate pitch until the clef-sign has been added

Stem The vertical component of a written note

Stress An accent

Stringendo Gradually faster

Subdominant The fourth note of a scale

Subito Suddenly

Submediant The sixth note of a scale

Syncopation Altering a regular stress-pattern to shift the accent to beats which are not normally stressed

Tablature Alternative systems of writing recorder music, which usually represent fingerings with signs to represent duration. Tablature has certain advantages over the normal system, among them that neither key-signature nor accidentals are required

Tacet Silent

Technique Usually, the mechanical ability required to play an instrument; skill

Tempo Literally, time. Often used to refer to speed

Tempo primo Resume original speed

Tenor blockflöte Tenor recorder

Tessitura The range of a part. Used most frequently by singers; instrumentalists are more likely to use 'register' or 'range'

Tipping Sometimes used for 'tonguing'. Sometimes, particularly in the early nineteenth century, a short sharp tonguing

Tonality Sometimes used for 'key'

Tone Two semitones; the quality of a sound. Sometimes used for 'note'

Tonguing Using the tongue as a valve for the column of air

Tonic The first note of a scale

Tranquillo Tranquil

Trill A rapid alternation of two notes

Triplet Three notes played in the time of two or four

Unison All parts play the same tune at the same pitch or in octaves

Vibrato A regular undulation of pitch and/or volume

Vivace Lively, quick

Volti subito Turn over quickly

Window Sometimes, the opening in the front of a recorder which contains or frames the knife-edge

Windway The narrow channel which leads and adjusts the player's breath against the knife-edge

Index

TEACH YOURSELF BOOKS

THE PIANO

King Palmer

This book does not claim to teach the reader to become an accomplished pianist, but rather to provide sufficient information and instruction for the beginner to learn to play with confidence and enjoyment.

Both the theory of piano music and the principles of the instrument are explained in the first chapters on the assumption that some readers will know nothing of either. The book then takes the reader through the technique and practice of piano playing, discussing such problems as fingering and phrasing, and advising the student on how to develop his skill.

A thorough and practical guide to the theory and practice of piano playing, invaluable both to the complete beginner and to the student.

ISBN 0 340 05688 6

TEACH YOURSELF BOOKS

MUSIC

King Palmer

Through radio, television and recordings, music of a very high standard is available today in a way it has never been before. Where the making of music is concerned, however, many people are discouraged by these same high standards and by the practical difficulties involved in getting started.

This book is designed to smooth out these problems by providing a guide simple enough to be understood by those with little previous knowledge of music, yet comprehensive enough to give a 'bird's eye view' of the entire field. Among the topics covered you will find explanations of musical notations and how music developed, introductions to piano, string, wind, organ and singing techniques, advice on choosing an instrument, how to practise, training your ear and musical appreciation.

This is a book for all those who want an *entrée* into the world of music and advice on how to pursue their particular interests.

ISBN 0 340 05666 5

TEACH YOURSELF BOOKS

☐ 21517 8	**Ballet** Ian Woodward	£2.95
☐ 16197 3	**The Guitar** Dale Fradd	£2.25
☐ 12456 3	**Jazz Piano** Eddie Harvey	£1.25
☐ 05666 5	**Music** King Palmer	£1.50
☐ 21847 9	**Opera** Robin May	£1.50
☐ 05688 6	**The Piano** King Palmer	75p

All these books are available at your local bookshop or news-agent, or can be ordered direct from the publisher. Just tick the titles you want and fill in the form below.

Prices and availability subject to change without notice.

....

TEACH YOURSELF BOOKS, P.O. Box 11, Falmouth, Cornwall.

Please send cheque or postal order, and allow the following for postage and packing:

U.K. – One book 22p plus 10p per copy for each additional book ordered, up to a maximum of 82p.

B.F.P.O. and EIRE – 22p for the first book plus 10p per copy for the next 6 books, thereafter 4p per book.

OTHER OVERSEAS CUSTOMERS – 30p for the first book and 10p per copy for each additional book.

Name ....

Address ....

....